Old Troubadour

Old Troubadour

Carl Sandburg with his Guitar Friends

Written and illustrated by

Gregory d'Alessio

Walker and Company New York

First published in the United States of America
in 1987 by the Walker Publishing Company, Inc.

Published simultaneously in Canada by Thomas Allen & Son
Canada, Limited, Markham, Ontario.

Book design: Laura Ferguson

Library of Congress Cataloging-in-Publication Data

d'Alessio, Gregory.
Old troubador.

Includes index.
1. Sandburg, Carl, 1878–1967. 2. Folk singers—
United States—Biography. I. Title.
ML420.S215D3 1987 784.4'924 [B] 87-2042
ISBN 0-8027-0966-4

Printed in the United States of America
10 9 8 7 6 5 4 3 2 1

The author and publisher wish to thank the following sources for use of reprinted
material in Old Troubadour:

Harcourt Brace Jovanovich, for permission to reprint these works:
"Cartoon," from Cornhuskers (Chapter Fifteen)
"Halsted Street Car," from Chicago Poems (Chapter Fifteen)
"Finish," from Smoke and Steel (Chapter Twenty-Six)
from The People, Yes (Chapter One)
from The Letters of Carl Sandburg (edited by Herbert Mitgang)
from Rootabaga Stories
from Bitter Summer Thoughts
The Guitar Review, for many quotes and illustrations.

United Media, for permission to reprint the Peanuts cartoon in Chapter Fifteen.

The Carl Sandburg Family Trust, Maurice C. Greenbaum and Frank M. Parker,
Trustees, for permission to reprint, "Art: Eleven Experimental Definitions," in
Chapter Fifteen.

To my wife, Terry,
who could have written this book herself.

Contents

Acknowledgments

THREE OR FOUR YEARS into the compilation of this memoir, someone asked me how it was coming along. "It's about 17/4ths finished," I answered. In bulk, weight, and number of pages, I was closing in on the record set by Sandburg's blockbuster *War Years*—all four volumes.

I knew it had to be cut, but it was some time before I could bring myself to part with a single sentence.

Good fortune later brought a charming young lady to Henderson Place. Penelope Niven paid us a call as Director of the Carl Sandburg Oral History Project. Ms. Niven is also Co-Director of the Carl Sandburg Collection Development Project. These organizations are jointly sponsored by the National Parks Service and the University of Illinois Library. When the University of Illinois Press suddenly showed a modest interest in my manuscript, Penelope Niven volunteered to choose an excerpt for the Press's consideration. I also owe her my deep thanks for subsequently cutting my work down to a size which a publisher might reasonably be expected to read and evaluate. She was the first editor of *Old Troubadour,* for which I am very appreciative.

Penelope Niven is currently working on a biography of Carl

Acknowledgements

Sandburg, sponsored in part by the National Endowment for the Humanities. Her biography should be published in 1988.

My further thanks to Philip Turner, editor at Walker and Company, who sensed an opening in the book world for biographical materials on Sandburg, and brought *Old Troubadour* into its present form.

More thanks go to Doris Frankel and Olga Steckler for their magic fingers, keen eyes, and mental telepathy in unscrambling (for free) my handwriting, which, at first glance, resembles Da Vinci's.

My thanks to:

Photographer Len Steckler for the generous usage of a collection of priceless Sandburg photos, never before published. We are all especially indebted to Lenny for being there to snap these pictures, simply for the joy of those moments; more for pleasure than treasure.

All who participated in those box-car days and nights so unforgettable; for those who are mentioned in these pages, but especially those whose names are lost in the maze on the cutting room floor.

The family—Paula Sandburg and daughters, Margaret Sandburg and Helga Crile for their warm encouragement over the years.

Joe Wershba for keeping the lines of communication open in the final years of Sandburg's life.

Last of all, my thanks to my agent Julian Bach, whose faith, supportive encouragement, and persistent effort have finally brought this book to you, the reader.

"Carl, dear old troubadour!"
—Frank Lloyd Wright

Introduction

Carl Sandburg, Old Troubadour

SENECA, THE STOIC PHILOSOPHER, statesman, and play-wright, said, "Men do not care how nobly they can live, but how long, although it is within the power of every man to live nobly, but within no man's power to live long."

Carl Sandburg had it both ways. He lived eighty-nine years, and he lived them nobly. His simple humanity, easy accessibility, love for family and friends, and fundamental integrity marked his private as well as his public life.

Back in 1922 Sandburg wrote a book of children's stories for his three daughters, Margaret, Janet, and Helga. He was forty-four years old, a husband for fourteen years, and a scrivener-father keen on providing the best for his little girls. Adults liked his kid stories, too, among them Frank Lloyd Wright, who called them the geatest work Sandburg ever did.

Years later, in 1957, when Wright was eighty-eight and Sandburg was seventy-nine, the two old friends sat for a joint interview conducted by Virginia Pasley of *Newsday,* in which Wright reaffirmed his affection for Sandburg's work. Sandburg had called Wright "the biggest Goddam Architek of 'em all." How did Wright address Carl?

Did he say Old Poet, Old Historian, Old Scrivener, Old Friend? No, instead he chose a name which embraced all of Carl Sandburg. He called him Old Troubadour.

Audiences across the country could recognize the silhouette of Sandburg with guitar, Sandburg singing, Sandburg the Troubadour. There was no unruly sea on the face of the earth that Carl Sandburg could not quell with a simple wave of his gnarled brown hand over a guitar, breaking into song in his soft baritone. He would sing and play all night if you let him.

It is said that nature has a way of telling a man when to slow down; but as the years went by, nature seemed to tell Carl to speed up. The decades of his seventies and eighties were incredibly busy. Through the new medium of television he became an instantly recognized national figure, America's bard and folk singer. He received honorary college degrees, had schools named for him, addressed Congress, accepted awards, made records, wrote for Hollywood, and made appearances on recital stages and at formal dinners reciting his poetry, singing his songs, and playing his guitar with those strong, loving hands.

Carl entered his seventies in 1948, the year he and I met. When he was eighty-two, Carl looked back on the decade of his seventies and declared to his friend and biographer Harry Golden that those were the years of some of his best work.

Carl looked back on the year 1948 with some anguish, however. His novel of the American Dream, *Remembrance Rock,* was not well received by the critics. A projected trip to Hollywood to help plan the book as a film was scuttled. Carl was disappointed by the critical reviews of *Remembrance Rock,* but demonstrated his customary keen good humor and a healthy resilience. He wrote to his old friend Fanny Butcher, "Sometimes I wonder how and why I am ambulant and in my right mind, enjoying fool songs more than ever."

It was the "fool songs" which began our friendship. In 1948 Carl Sandburg looked up the New York guitar crowd. He came to us at the chronological age of seventy, although physically he looked no more than fifty and spiritually he was even younger than that. Sandburg was eager to do something about his great infatuation with the guitar. He wanted to get to know other guitarists and to learn from them. On occasion he was moved to write poems to the guitar. Its music and the guitar people who shared the music were for Carl a constant source of fellowship and fun. Yet outside the circle of his new-found guitar friends, this salutary, rejuvenating experience in his life went singularly unnoticed. Curiously, his colleagues in the writing profession and the news media overlooked the light side of Sandburg, so vital a part of his sanity, humor, and humanity.

Journalist and author Herbert Mitgang saw the significance of the guitar and its people while he was editing *The Letters of Carl Sandburg* (Harcourt Brace & World, 1968). When Mitgang asked for a look at my cache of Sandburg letters, I bade him come to my home on Henderson Place in New York. Mitgang read all of the letters and studied the many sketches I had made of Carl.

A few days after his visit, Mitgang wrote me, "No wonder Carl liked Henderson Place. He saw artistry and human qualities (warmth and humor) there. That, he always had an instinct for. . . . His letters to you show still another side of Carl—the guitar friends. . . ."

Carl said that the years of his seventies were the times of his best work. I like to think my noble friend might have also said that his seventies were the years of some of his best times.

Henderson Place

LATE ON A RAINY SATURDAY afternoon in the spring of 1959, I dashed to a taxi miraculously vacated at the northwest corner of Madison Avenue and Fifty-seventh Street. I had been gallery-hopping all day, and now I had to get home fast.

"To Henderson Place and drive like hell!" I ordered the driver crisply.

Outside of giving me a baleful look, my driver ignored the whimsy. Clearly he'd never read the Benchley story about the scholarly chap who bounded into an old battered brougham at the Plaza and boomed out, "To the Museum of Natural History and drive like hell!" Throwing motor and meter into gear, he whooshed off along wet Madison Avenue.

If you drive too fast along East Eighty-sixth Street between York and East End Avenues—or even if you walk too fast and fail to look north—you'll miss our street. To call it an alley is a calumny, as it is wide enough for three car-widths, even if it is closed at one end. Calling it an enclave would place too aloof a connotation upon it, and besides, we are not that secluded physically or socially from the city beyond. A mews, perhaps? Certainly not now; nor is it known that it ever was one. I've just looked up cul-de-sac, and I guess that is closest to the kind of a place Henderson Place is.

Our house is one of six on the very short street. Opposite us, on its west side, once squatted the old Misericordia Hospital. The site is now crammed with two huge cooperative buildings. Prior to their looming presence, a row of three-story houses stood there, of the same vintage and architecture as our house, with matching brick of the russet patina which only years of exposure can impart. These modest structures served as the student nurses' quarters of the hospital nearby. There was no traffic along the street. The only vehicles in sight were the six cars belonging to the six owners on our side. Opposite were the hospital limousines, operated by tiny nuns of the Misericordia Order.

We call Henderson Place home, Terry and I. Theresa Hilda, my wife, the Missus, if you will. Not until I heard Carl Sandburg call his wife the Missus did I start calling mine the Missus, too.

In another taxi years later in 1967, on another rainy day not long after Carl Sandburg's death, I was in no humor to pull the "drive like hell" gambit on my driver. To avoid confusion or misunderstanding, I gave the cabby my destination. I omitted the specific name Henderson Place. Instead I gave out a general direction: Eighty-sixth Street, between York and East End.

Automatically, the driver took a precise, direct course. I settled back into my seat. Now we were going east along Eighty-sixth Street and passing York Avenue.

"Henderson Place," I said. "Just ahead, to the left, before East End." The cabby nosed us slightly into the street. As I was paying him, he said, somewhat hurt, "Say, mister, why dincha say Henderson Place in the first place? I woulda known where it was, because I been here before. You know who lives in that middle house?" He pointed to ours. "I took this old fella there one night; Carl Sanborne, the poet. I seen him on TV once with Gene Kelly. Reckanized him right away."

Well, Carl Sandburg was never a landed resident of Henderson Place, but he did live on the street from time to time. He was our house guest often in the middle and late 1950s, and in 1957 actually made our home his New York headquarters for a month.

The driver remembered the white-thatched, friendly poet who had shown him how to find Henderson Place. Thanks to television, he had recognized a poet, even if he'd never read any of his works.

I have not emphasized one characteristic of Henderson Place as a New York street distinguishing it from virtually all others: it is private. Not a nice word, if you knew Carl and his fiercely libertarian, if not anarchical, fulminations against private property. At least this was Sandburg's position in 1936 when he wrote *The People Yes,* including this excerpt:

> *"Get off this estate."*
> *"What for?"*
> *"Because it's mine."*
> *"Where did you get it?"*
> *"From my father."*
> *"Where did he get it?"*
> *"From his father."*
> *"And where did he get it?"*
> *"He fought for it."*
> *"Well, I'll fight you for it."*

But any reluctance to be housed on a private street as a violation of his principles didn't seem to bother Carl. Perhaps he had mellowed. In any event, he wasn't the least concerned, for he saw soon enough that our so-called "privacy" was but an amusing euphemism. Squatters boldly sneaked their cars into the street and parked them wherever they could find a space, sometimes leaving them snugly slumbering for weeks at a time in their stolen nests.

Carl Sandburg said the most hated word in the English language is "exclusive." He boomed it out with a withering gusto when he said it, lingering on the middle syllable: "Exclooooooooosive!" It poured out ominously from his pursed lips, as a Biblical prophet might have pronounced doom upon the sinful nation. But Henderson Place was never in any danger of his condemnation. Our kind of exclusiveness was not only inoffensive to him, but knee-slappingly amusing.

However, Henderson Place does possess a unique kind of privacy that even the scorn of Carl Sandburg could do little about: its weather. Our street has a weather all its own. No matter that the wind just outside our cul-de-sac is slack, a mini-hurricane could be raging within. During a blizzard, our private winds can mischievously funnel snow through a keyhole; rain strikes our house at a ninety-degree angle, ingeniously squirreling its way through the interstices of the brickwork and pouring proudly into our living room. Another very private wind which I call the Henderson Place Mistral banks snow up in huge mounds against the front door, from its top to the bottom, so that when you open it, you're staring at a wall of snow whose surface is an exact replica of the door, in reverse, like a sculptor's mold of a bas-relief complete with doorknob, lock mechanism, house number—even the knocker, in all its baroque details.

I write of our street with more than a modicum of modesty, even in excessive self-abasement, to avoid crowing and sounding smug and property-proud; for Henderson Place is actually a street oozing with charm, a New York City landmark, and an ideal place to live, if you must live in a teeming, perilous city. It is quiet, gracious, sequestered from the hustle and bustle of traffic and other disturbances. And the neighbors are tops. (Archibald MacLeish, Edmund Wilson, Gilbert Seldes, and even John Barrymore resided at different times on this street, long before the Missus and I moved here and Carl Sandburg came to call.) Our neighbors breed red-headed angels, and the street is always full of another generation of cherubim.

Despite its brevity, spring would be the most welcome time of the year. This was the time when we welcomed Carl Sandburg to New York and Henderson Place, where he was often our house guest.

One April day, beginning his first stay, Sandburg climbed the five steps up our old and weatherworn brownstone stoop. He arrived at 8 Henderson Place in his seventy-eighth year. Standing there at the open door, he held in each hand a bulging shopping bag, their weight shown in the rigidity of his arms, the tautness of the bag handles, and the prominence of the veins standing out on the tops of his brown-freckled hands. The "luggage" contained all of his needs for a longish stay: shirts (all white but one, which was a heavy plaid), long johns, socks, hankies; and for his immediate needs, a dozen oranges, a quart of goat's milk, a fifth of Jack Daniels, and books. He had reading and writing and work to do. He would work out of Henderson Place, with Catherine McCarthy, of Harcourt Brace, his publishers. Our house would be his headquarters.

Carl fell in love with our street—its simplicity, its old-world charm, its quiet. He noted with pleasure our pretty little Carl Schurz Park (filled with evocations of his beloved Lincoln), just a few steps to the east. He liked parks, he said, where people can relax, and ours especially, for it overlooked a river. He put it down for an early, extended exploration.

I would venture to guess that it was none of these virtues of our house and street that made him choose us, though; it was the presence of guitars, the anticipation of meeting guitarists, of long "boxcar" evenings, parties, and singing. And he certainly found them here. Sandburg was enthralled with the guitar and its catalytic power to consolidate all the ingredients of a party into a homogeneous good time.

Any friend of Carl Sandburg's who ever was his host knows that as a house guest, he was no problem. You found out quickly how easy he was to feed, to entertain; you saw how well he could take care of himself, how Spartan were his needs. Then your anxiety to make good as the host of a truly great man faded away.

He made *you* feel at home.

The Sandburg Room

WHEN I BROKE THE NEWS to the Missus of Carl Sandburg's first overnight stay at Henderson Place, she went all panicky.

"Where'll we put him?"

"On the top floor, of course," I answered.

"But—those stairs! He can't make those stairs," she remonstrated.

"We'll see, we'll see," I said. "Let's leave it up to him when he arrives. I do know that he's a great walker."

Healthy and hardy though Sandburg seemed to be, I nevertheless shared the Missus's anxiety; scaling the heights of our house might be hazardous for an octogenarian. Even for me, then a quaking quintogenarian, the thirty-eight-step climb was not exactly mounting a molehill.

When Carl arrived, I offered him the top floor, but added that if the stairs intimidated him, we could easily make arrangements for his comfort in other parts of the house. When he saw the light, airy rooms, four of them, remote from the rest of the house, he said it was the place for him.

"Those steps," he assured us, "don't worry about them at all. We got 'em at home—no problem. Nothin' wrong with the old ticker, y'know. I gotta method of climbin' stairs when there's a lotta them.

Look." Then he showed us: first, one step up; then bring the other foot flat beside it. Stand there some five or ten seconds; repeat.

I knew that Sandburg could eat anything, drink anything. That would pose no problems on his visit to Henderson Place. Now I knew he could probably climb anything.

Soon Carl was settled in his quarters, his things spread about him, books open, books closed, some with small scraps of paper placed in different parts as markers. We were glad to see him happy and comfortable in his aerie. It was where we'd have wanted him to be; we were relieved, too, that it wasn't necessary to put him into a noisier part of the house, with one quarter as much room.

That there was nothing wrong with Carl's old ticker, in a clinical sense, was immediately demonstrated. He got to his rooms at the top, never once resorting to his "resting" method. He negotiated the thirty-eight steps with ease.

There was nothing wrong with the old ticker, either, as the seat and source of his inexhaustible humor, humanity, and soul. He was a joy to have around. He made us feel good; and when he would say to us from time to time, "You're not what's wrong with the world," we believed him.

One morning, as we were sitting around the breakfast table, Terry asked Carl to write something she could have inscribed on a bronze plaque for his fireplace.

I wondered if any great man ever wrote a memorial to himself and a place he slept in, writing it in the past tense while he was very much alive? Carl Sandburg was about to do it with gaiety. Almost before Terry popped the question, he was off. Without hem, haw, or hesitation, he gave her the legend immortalizing his occupancy of the Upstairs Bedroom of Henderson Place, U.S.A., Anno Domini 1957. Terry sat before him taking dictation, as if the boss had called to his secretary, "Miss Jones, take a plaque."

He settled back and gave the text: "They wanted me to have the highest room in the house," he intoned in the mock dramatics of one delivering deathless lines, "so they put me here. And if there had been a fifth floor or a sixth floor, they would have put me there. Carl Sandburg."

With dispatch, Terry delivered the words to the engraver's before the ink on the paper was dry. The plaque arrived by mail on the morning of Sandburg's departure for home in Flat Rock, North Carolina. He had left only ten minutes before. Before his bed was cold, Terry had the precious bronze slab secured for all time to the fireplace of what from then on we called The Sandburg Room.

A Distinguished Coterie

I FIRST MET CARL SANDBURG in 1948. On September twenty-third of that year, two days before my birthday, a phone call came from someone purporting to be Sandburg.

"I hope the guitar gang is free tonight. If so, what are the chances of getting together?" Never had I heard so resonant, measured, and beautiful a voice.

I sputtered something about how a group of us was indeed gathering that night at the Russian Yar restaurant in the first of a series of parties marking my birthday on the twenty-fifth.

"Sure," I said. "Drop over about nine o'clock. Do you know the city? It's on Fifty-second between Fifth and Sixth . . . just opposite Leon and Eddie's."

Of course I had heard of Carl Sandburg all my life; I had read two of his greatest poems—"Fog" and "Chicago." I knew he was an authentic folk singer, and I had heard some of his old records. I knew that Sandburg began to play the guitar and sing folk songs long before folk music was part of the American popular music picture. With little competition, Sandburg was possibly the most authentic troubadour of those times.

To my shame, however, in 1948, I thought he was already a part of the dim past, a legend revered as only heroes long gone are venerated.

Quickly, I called headquarters of The Society of the Classic Guitar, which also served as the studio of our president, Vladimir Bobri—artist, guitarist, and composer. Bobri, a Russian émigré from the Revolution, had arrived in New York in 1922. Our small group of guitar devotees had elected him president of the Society. It was Bobri himself who answered the phone.

"Some joker who says he's Carl Sandburg just called and says he wants to meet us," I laughed. "So I told him to drop in at the Yar tonight—okay?"

"Ah—so he called you, too," said Bobri in his rhythmic Russian accent. "Yes—yes—the same man called here earlier, and I told him to arrange something with you since you are the secretary. I do not believe it is Sandburg, either, but we shall see, we shall see."

At nine on the dot, a man appeared on the small landing just inside the door of the Russian Yar. A lick of white hair shone under his floppy dark fedora. He was tall, straight, and alert, with twinkling eyes and sprightly steps. He was dressed soberly in a dark blue serge suit, with touches of individuality: a carelessly but distinctively knotted bow tie and a silk scarf intricately arranged around his neck.

It was Carl Sandburg, all right.

I studied our man. I knew that he was in his seventieth year, and I was on the alert for any signs of fatigue or geriatric deterioration. Only his creamy white hair could stamp him as old, but it did not make him look old, only more beautiful. I remembered with embarrassment my earlier assumption that Sandburg was dead. Here he was, more alive than any of us at the table, younger than me by decades.

Before Sandburg found us, he said in an interview with the *Saturday Review of Literature:* "After five years' immersion in *Remembrance Rock,* I am eager to be with the guitar-playing gang—one of the most distinguished coteries in New York." *Coterie:* how that high-sounding word fitted us, I was at a loss to understand. It was a fancy word, and we were not fancy people. We were just a group of people who were hopelessly gone on the classic guitar—the *classic* guitar—not the jazz, steel-stringed guitar. I suppose from that point of view, we could be described as a coterie. But in the same sentence, Sandburg also called us "the guitar gang."

Gang or coterie, we were now assembled with Sandburg in our midst. Thus began his association with the classic guitar and its devoted followers. At seventy, he now had the time to explore this new world.

The Yar rang with music, guitar playing, and singing. Meanwhile, the vodka flowed. When there appeared the slightest void between surface of liquor and rim of glass, vigilant Vladimir Bobri, in clear Russian, snapped the waiters into action.

I wondered how Sandburg, the great American poet and biographer of Lincoln, was reacting to these Russian shenanigans. He sat for all those hours rocklike in his chair. His only movements were his drinking arm, his talking lips, his twinkling eyes, and the shifting, now and then, of his white hair when he turned his head from one of us to the other. At seventy, he was clearly sound of wind, limb, and digestion.

Of particular delight to Carl that evening was Eithne Golden, an Irish lass accomplished in languages and a fine guitarist-singer of songs from many ethnic backgrounds and origins, including the Eskimo. "Ethnic" Golden, a Society wag dubbed her. Certainly, Sandburg was taken immediately by her good looks, but when he heard her name, he complimented her upon her fine job of translating Andrés Segovia's autobiography *La Guitarra y Yo* (The Guitar and I), which was then running in our magazine, *The Guitar Review*. Nothing of the old-world charm of Segovia's exquisite Spanish was lost in Eithne's translation into equally exquisite English. Carl had caught its fidelity. He had met Segovia, and he knew how Segovia would write. When Eithne sang a song in Armenian, he was completely won. He had only to know that it was a folk song. It mattered little if he could not understand the words.

When the song ended, Carl, folk singer himself, was in awe. "Imagine that girl singing a song in Armenian. What a wonderful life she must have!" he said reverently.

When curfew arrived, all of us were well past the euphoria of the first dozen drinks. Only Carl was calm, contained, clear-eyed, and coherent. We spilled out of the yawning Yar, and said our good nights in the cool September pre-dawn of old Fifty-second Street. I asked the poet where he was staying while in town.

"At Batchelor's," he answered.

"C. D.? The *Daily News* editorial cartoonist?" I asked, making a wild stab at a possible happy coincidence, since I knew C. D. Batchelor well. In fact, we lived next door to each other in the Tudor

City section of New York, in the lower East Forties (this was in the days before Henderson Place).

"Right," Carl answered. "He's an old friend. He offers me his penthouse apartment—the Glass House, I call it—when I'm in town; and tonight he's out of town."

I was jubilant! We could share a cab. I looked anxiously along the emptiness of the street, hoping a cab would materialize out of the morning mist. In a few minutes, I thought with relief, still feeling a responsibility and solicitude for the old gentleman, I would have my charge safely home. In fact, my sense of obligation was still so strong, despite the apparent fitness of Sandburg, that I'd failed to note that if indeed anyone needed help, it was I. My vision was blurred, but I was able to see the gleam of headlights far to the west along Fifty-second Street and approaching rapidly. I rolled over to the middle of the road, frantically waving my arms.

"Let it go, Greg; let it go," Carl called from the curb. "We'll walk."

These, now, would be my first moments alone with Carl Sandburg—a walk that I knew would take no more than twenty minutes. My head began to clear.

I wished those precious minutes would last forever. Since then I have always recalled with deep nostalgic pleasure that walk along the clean, echoing streets of New York, in that gentle September dawn in 1948. With me was a man who had passed in the space of an evening from legend into reality and who would become my guitar pal for the rest of his life. Now I think of that dawn and the walk with sorrow, for the man is gone back into legend.

Carl walked rapidly that long-ago night. There was little talk; but fancied or real, I heard birds singing in the trees along the sleeping streets, even from the eaves and crannies of the buildings, as if in serenade to the poet walking in their precincts.

We arrived at my building, named in true Tudor tradition Hardwicke Hall. Carl handed me over to my elevator man standing at the entrance, taking in the dawn air. Then Carl continued to the next Tudor castle, Haddon Hall, and C. D. Batchelor's penthouse atop it. He stopped and turned to me. "Oh, wait a minute!" he said.

"My God!" I thought. "He wants me to join him in a nightcap!"

He led me inside my lobby. "I wonder if you have a spare guitar you could lend me," he said. "Before I turn in, I always like to sing a song or two."

4

Segovia and Sandburg: Maestro and Pupil

CARL SANDBURG CARRIED ON a love affair with the guitar for most of his adult life. The classic guitar is a demanding instrument, and it always eluded his eager but unsophisticated fingers. Resigned to that hard fact early in the courtship, he was content to accept the status of friend of the family, or doting uncle. After all, hadn't he already wooed and won his first love, poetry?

Sandburg was first smitten with the classic guitar in the mid-thirties. He had just heard a recording by Andrés Segovia, and he marveled over the beauty of the timbres, subtleties, and nuances that came from the graceful instrument. In those days, Segovia played a gut-stringed guitar; all classic guitars were so fitted before 1945, when the nylon string took over. Sandburg's own guitar was lyre-shaped with steel strings, capable of only a metallic twang. The music of Segovia's sweet guitar won the poet's heart. He wanted to meet the great master of this unpretentious instrument which miraculously gave off polyphonic music, replete with basses, trebles, and counterpoint.

Segovia fully possesses the instrument. He hypnotizes it to the will;

draws from it spellbinding voices and colors. He is a great instrumentalist, but first, a great musician.

Sandburg, eager to get closer to the classic guitar, realized that he would first have to meet Segovia. When his chance came he nearly missed it. In May 1938, he was invited to a party, and he almost didn't go.

In those days, the home of Dr. and Mrs. J. R. Buchbinder in Chicago was the gathering place of artists, writers, musicians, and intellectuals in many fields. Hazel Felman Buchbinder, composer, folklorist, and collaborator with Carl Sandburg on the collection of folk songs *The American Songbag,* had known the poet well before 1927, when the book was first published. She had also entertained Segovia after all his concert dates in Chicago. While the poet and the guitarist had heard of each other, they had not met, and although she tried, Mrs. Buchbinder could never get the two together.

Hazel admitted to me that she almost failed again on May 21, 1938. Carl at first refused her invitation to meet the famous British biographer and historian Philip Guedalla, in whose honor she had announced a cocktail-tea party. Many historians and newspaper people were also expected. A newspaperman himself and also an historian—he was but two years away from the Pulitzer Prize for his *Abraham Lincoln: The War Years*—Sandburg said he was not unwilling to mingle with the latter gentry. As for Guedalla, he snorted, "I don't like the fellow's book on Palmerston. I'm not coming."

But now Hazel threw out some sure-fire bait. "You've always wanted to meet Segovia, haven't you? Well, did you know that he's playing in Chicago this evening? And what if I were to tell you that he is coming here after his concert?"

"Listen," Carl boomed. "I will go to that concert myself—I didn't know he was playing—I'll pick up Segovia, and we'll come to your supper together!"

If joyful anticipation was in the air at the party, there was also tension. On that day, May 2, 1938, Hitler's Nazis marched into the city of Vienna, placing all of Austria under their domination. Although the events of that day were unfolding over three thousand miles away, it was nevertheless very close to Chicago and the party in progress. One of the guests, Lloyd Lewis of the *Chicago Daily News,* stayed close to the telephone. He had an open wire with his correspondent in

Vienna and relayed to the guests his man's eye-witness account of the developments in the history-making crisis, right up to the actual entrance of the Nazi hordes into the old city.

Meanwhile, another historical march was developing on that fateful day—a happier and more felicitous one, compared to the ominous stirrings of World War II then taking place in Austria. The tension of that drama was broken when Sandburg and Segovia, arm in arm, marched into the Buchbinder apartment, smiling and already old friends. The association, thus begun, lasted longer than Nazi Austria by twenty-two years, ending only with the death of Carl Sandburg in July 1967.

Sandburg and Segovia turned to their common love—music—and curiously enough, Carl was eager to make music first. He couldn't wait to begin singing for the Maestro, leading off with perhaps the most untranslatable song in the American folk idiom, "Sam Hall." A Spaniard, Segovia's second language was French. His English was limited in those days, so the lyrics of the violent song were explained to the Maestro by a few guests who could speak French.

How do you translate into French, or any language for that matter, the violence and rage in the line, "God damn your eyes!"—especially as Carl used to sing it, with his great sense of drama and poetry?

Carl was perhaps the most satisfying party guest a hostess could ask for. He never needed to be urged to sing or say his poetry; he just had to be allowed. He was always quick to pick up his guitar and raise his voice in song. "He just never doesn't feel like singing, that's all," Mrs. Buchbinder said.

Segovia, on the other hand, rarely plays at social gatherings. In a small intimate group where the guitar is uppermost in everyone's attention and conversation, he might sometimes take the instrument from a struggling devotee and give a corrective demonstration that is inevitably a performance; but unlike Julian Bream, who likes to play some relaxing jazz at a party, or Alirio Diaz, who never refuses to spin out a rousing Venezuelan dance or any other kind of rhythmic music on his guitar, the sternly disciplined Segovia is like a severe parent in his protection of the purity of the classic guitar. He is never so "corrupted" by music in its actual, primitive folk form. He is no strummer, or twanger, or thumper; although he comes from Andalusia, where flamenco was born, he will suggest the flamenco idiom only when it is woven into a piece by a composer or arranger for the classic guitar—often himself.

Instead of playing, he prefers to talk, and he can, brilliantly, wittily. He has *done* his playing for the day, only a few hours before in a concert hall. His guitar has been laid away, secure in its case, back in his hotel room, to be reopened in the next morning for his daily practice of several hours.

It is a wise hostess who takes the trouble to check out the areas of privacy and prerogatives of a distinguished guest. Mrs. Buchbinder knew Segovia well enough, or thought she did, and therefore kept mum in the request department.

But a female guest, naive in the ways of such party protocol, piped up innocently: "Please, Mr. Segovia—won't *you* play something for us now?" The Buchbinders went into semi-shock and then into full shock when the maestro, without hesitation, agreed. He would be delighted to return some of the pleasure just given him by the singing poet. The warmth and simplicity of Sandburg's music affected the guitarist; even Carl's crude but fittingly uncomplicated two-finger playing was endearing to Segovia for its honesty and lack of pretension. Quickly, someone arranged to pick up Segovia's guitar at the hotel, and soon after, Sandburg, watching Segovia from a distance of only two or three feet, saw *how it was done*. He began to understand the discipline involved, the years of practice required to master the instrument so that the attention of the artist may focus entirely on the music, without concern for or distraction of technique to block the path. Carl must have known in his heart that he could never muster the discipline required for the classic guitar when he had books to write, poems to compose, and many other pressing duties.

About ten years after that first meeting with Segovia, Carl said to me wistfully: "I'm sure that Segovia had never met anyone so deeply loving of the guitar and nevertheless so faithless in his love."

Childlike, Carl was overcome with wonder by Segovia's magical skill. It was a fascinating example of dexterity and theatrics, a demonstration of perfect coordination of hand, ear, and tactile sense that Segovia brought to the guitar. With uncanny accuracy, he could retune a string gone sour in a fraction of a second. Sandburg's first encounter with this feat of speed was when Segovia pulled it on Sandburg. Preparing to sing his songs to Segovia, Carl tuned his guitar and was ready to play, or thought he was. But Segovia was sitting on the far side of the room.

"He shook his head," Mrs. Buchbinder recalls, "and smiling, he rose, walked over to Carl, flicked at the tuning pegs for a split second each, patted Carl's ear lovingly, and without breaking his stride, returned to his seat."

Not only this feat, but all of Segovia's mannerisms on the concert stage delighted Sandburg no end. It was hard to believe, he often said to me after a concert, that this stout fellow, hunched so ungracefully over his guitar, could produce such graceful music. Picture the instrument: frail, severe in design. See the left foot of the artist raised upon a small Louis Quinze footstool, brocaded and intricately carved. The waist of the guitar fits snugly over a plump thigh; plump fingers like tiny, overweight ballet dancers do their choreography on the strings. The swift left hand, with a life of its own, moves knowingly along the fingerboard. The strings willingly swoon with delight, sing with joy, yield their most precious gifts of response before the pressure of fingers. The fingers of the other hand do their work secretly behind the broad wall of the metacarpals. Hear the incredible speed, the nuance of tone, the subtlety of color.

"What's goin' on behind that fist?" Carl would whisper.

Segovia's face is inscrutable, except for some vague, barely perceptible movements of his eyebrows; his eyes seem expressionless behind thick-lensed spectacles. He is an immobile, phlegmatic figure—graven upon his chair; his eyes are fastened on his left hand only, never on the audience. There is neither smile nor scowl to betray emotion.

In a twinkling—like a sudden gust of wind breaking the shape and outlines of a tree—the contours of the silhouette upon the stage are altered. In midstream of a number, usually a vigorous one, Segovia's sharp ear tells him that a string needs to be tuned; it has lost its grip at the tuning head. Under the lusty playing, it is giving up, going flat. Segovia betrays, by the slightest shift of his eyes from fingers to tuning peg, his awareness of the impending problem, which, to less of a master, would be a disaster.

If I were at the concert with Sandburg, he would nudge me. "Here it comes!" he would say.

Without any change in the tempo of the music or the movement of the fingers on his right hand, in the split second between the fingering of one fret to the next, be it a half- or thirty-second note, Segovia's left hand would leave the fingerboard and flash up to the tuning peg, give it a quick twist, and return just as swiftly to the job of fingering. No other concert instrument but the guitar can be so adjusted while the music is actually being played upon it.

No other instrumentalist can do it with the ease and aplomb of Segovia.

When Sandburg and Segovia made their fond farewells after the Buchbinder party, they vowed to keep the friendship going. The Maestro promised to help Sandburg with his guitar playing. "You have a good touch," he said, "and with some training, you can make a good improvement, especially to learn a few more chords." Sandburg's repertoire of chords, which he played two-finger style, was confined basically to the keys of A and C.

"I will send you a few exercises in other keys to practice," Segovia continued, "and sometime we will actually sit down to a lesson." All this was spoken, of course, in very broken English or translated Spanish. But Sandburg understood.

His cup ran over. Carl went to his mailbox every day and looked for the promised piece of music. Each time he was disappointed. Segovia, deep in his flourishing concert career, was too busy to think up a simple chord exercise. There was complicated music to write or transcribe, then to practice, and then to play on stage or to record. Thus, Sandburg was not yet the pupil of Segovia.

Twelve years later, Sandburg received his first lesson. He could now say, "I am a pupil of Segovia." And few if any could yet say that, since Segovia did not begin formal teaching until a few years later in Siena, Italy.

Again, it was Hazel Buchbinder who brought Carl and Segovia together. On a family visit to Havana in March 1950, Hazel was happy to find that Segovia was appearing with the Havana Philharmonic Orchestra. Remembering the disappointed Carl back home, Hazel had dinner with Segovia and reminded him of the lesson promised twelve years earlier.

Segovia summoned a waiter, saying, "Some note paper, please." The waiter promptly brought him hotel stationery. "Bueno," said Carl's teacher, and with flowery calligraphy he then and there penned the lesson, a simple scale, including the correct fingering for the left hand. He inscribed it: "For my dear Sandburg—to teach his fingers as if they were little children." He handed it to Hazel and instructed her to deliver it to Carl in person.

Hazel reported, "Carl couldn't begin to understand the lessons." Segovia's flamboyant baroque flourishes floored him, for one thing; also, his knowledge of music notation was negligible, and his willing fingers were not able to articulate the notes, even if he could read them.

But he always treasured the manuscript.

Although Carl chose the guitar years before as the accompanying instrument to his songs, he never attained the skills of a soloist despite his "lessons" with Segovia. But he was a good listener and a delight to all players. Carl's ear was keen, and his eye critical and sharp. Mediocre playing never got past him. At a concert one night we were listening to a new guitarist on the New York scene. Fruitlessly he tried to emulate Segovia's phlegmatic playing manner—that body, a graven form—the face expressionless with only an eyebrow flicking upward at times, even the hands immobile—only the fingers hidden by his ham of a fist, busy on the strokes. The new guitarist's playing left much to be desired.

"He plays with an economy of body movement," whispered Carl, "but with a greater economy of talent."

The Guitar Review

CARL SANDBURG WAS EAGER to meet the New York guitar crowd. Thus on a September night in 1948 he joined "the distinguished coterie," as he called us, to partake liberally of guitar, song, food, wine, and camaraderie. He was the honored guest at the feast.

The members of The Society of the Classic Guitar soon learned that Carl was not merely a loving elderly gentleman looking for a good party.

No! What really brought him to us was our magazine, *The Guitar Review.*

He wanted to write for us.

"Do you know," I asked him, "that The Society of the Classic Guitar and *The Guitar Review* are among the most successful nonprofit ventures in the land? What I mean is that, of all the nonprofit ventures, our profit is more *non* than any of the others."

He chuckled. "I know. I've read your masthead many times. You don't pay for material. But I've got one or two guitar things that might go in the *Review,* and one of the things I want out of life is to get what I write printed."

It was our magazine that first came to his attention. It was what he liked about us. We were a modest, albeit esoteric, publication then, of some four or five hundred circulation. The classic guitar, much less

The Guitar Review, had a long way to go before attaining the popular acceptance it enjoys now.

At the Yar, on the historic night of our first meeting, Carl lifted his glass high in the gesture of a toast, and out of the blue, in clear mellifluous syllables and with a loving regard for how accents fell, this famous American poet recited one by one, with dramatic pauses, the very unfamous, unsung names of the editors of *The Guitar Review.*

Carl's feat was the high point of our evening and the more impressive because it was truly spontaneous, unadorned admiration for an effort that he knew to be a labor of love.

Sandburg liked what we were doing. He said, "You fellers deserve salutations and deep thanks for *The Guitar Review.* . . . I shall treasure its issues wherein you so properly and intelligently honor that noble instrument."

By hook or crook we were turning out a magazine—a beautiful one, too, and not one of us was a professional editor, writer, musician, musicologist, or scholar. However, in one department we excelled. Since most of us were artists, we possessed the know-how of putting together a book with taste as to choice of fine papers, excellent artwork, typography, and imaginative layout. Vladimir Bobri, George Giusti, Antonio Petruccelli, Grisha Dotzenko, Karl Noel, and Saul Marantz were crack artists drawing down good yearly incomes but hopelessly hooked on the guitar and willing to work on *The Guitar Review* for nothing. We had the expert advice of Franz Hess, a typographer of city-wide fame. I was jack-of-all-trades—proofreader, letter-writer, caption-writer, associate editor, and occasional spot-cartoon supplier. We made an unbeatable team. Every moment of our spare time was spent over drafting tables, typewriters, drawing boards, proofs, and at the typographer's or the lithographer's, since *The Guitar Review* was an offset production. We even won a Graphic Arts Certificate of Excellence. A curious study in anomaly was to see our exhibit at the Magazine Show in 1950 in juxtaposition with the florid extrovert, *Ladies' Home Journal*—"circulation 2,000,000." And beside it, the modest *Guitar Review,* "circulation 800."

Andrés Segovia was our honorary president. No mere letterhead honorary president. He *worked* for us, contributing pedagogical pieces to *The Guitar Review,* advising us as to the choice of music, even beginning to write his autobiography for first publication in our fledgling magazine. Unfortunately, as his career burgeoned, he picked up the scrivener's pen less and less, and his guitar more and more, carrying it to every corner of the world that eagerly awaited his unique and precious art.

Busy as he was, though, he found time not only to help with material for *The Guitar Review,* but also to keep it from actually going under.

In 1950, we were facing financial disaster. A big printer's bill was staring us in the face. Our money, much of it made up of donations from our own pockets to get the magazine started, had run out. Sadly, we realized that after only a few years, the promise of an American classic guitar magazine—the only American classic guitar magazine—would end up as a wistful dream.

But Maestro Andrés Segovia came to our rescue with a benefit concert. It netted us a thousand dollars. We were back on our feet, to flourish for many more years.

The Segovia contribution to *The Guitar Review* which unquestionably lured Sandburg into our fold was the gift of a few installments of the Maestro's autobiography, which appeared in its early issues.

Originally written in Spanish, the old-world charm of Segovia's elegant prose enchanted Carl just as fully as did the great music. Having known and admired Segovia as a musician ever since they met in 1938, Carl was delighted and proud to greet his friend as a writer now. If he could not join him in a guitar duet, he could at least try to hold his own with Andrés as a writer for *The Guitar Review,* and he was anxious to start without delay.

Carl was soon calling *The Guitar Review* "our" magazine. He did so casually in a letter which included a clipping from the *London Times,* a piece on the classic guitar and its master, Andrés Segovia. "Herewith and hereby," he wrote,

> *you may know the guitar is found in The Lunnon Times to be an iggstrawnery instrument—iggstrawnery, old chap. Still and all it may make a filler for our righteously proud journal.*
>
> yr obdt svt
>
> Carlo

On December 29, 1949, Carl wrote me: "Zeal is what you and Bobri and all the rest have. Zeal is what lovers, crusaders, and fanatics have. Having zeal makes you a zealot. Seldom is a zealot a helot, but we won't go into that now. . . ."

In a 1951 issue specially devoted to the song and guitar, our newest contributor offered this stunner about our mutually beloved instrument:

THE GUITAR
Some definitions by Carl Sandburg

A chattel with a soul often in part owning its owner
  and tantalizing him with his lack of perfection.
An instrument of quaint form and quiet demeanor
  dedicated to the dulcet rather than the diapason.
A box of chosen wood having intimate accessories
  wherefrom sound may be measured and commanded
  to the interest of ears not lost to hammer crash
  or wind whisper.
A portable companion distinguished from the piano
  in that you can take it with you,
  neither horses nor motor truck being involved.
A small friend weighing less than a newborn infant,
  ever responsive to all sincere efforts
  aimed at mutual respect, depth of affection
  or love gone off the deep end.
A device in the realm of harmonic creation
  where six silent strings have the sound potential
  of profound contemplation or happy go lucky whim.
A highly evolved contrivance whereby delicate
  melodic moments mingle with punctuation of silence
  bringing "the creative hush."
A vibratory implement under incessant practice
  and skilled cajolery giving out with serene
  maroon meditations, flame dancers in scarlet sashes,
  snow-white acrobats plunging into black midnight pools,
  odd numbers in evening green waltzing
  with even numbers in dawn pink.

The other manuscript was a breezy piece about the guitar in his own life:

CONFESSION

By Carl Sandburg

The present writer submits the hazy and hazardous definitions (earlier in this issue) rather than a report or a series of observations on his experiences in the use of the guitar for the accompaniment of songs. I can testify under oath, of course, that the guitar never betrays a singer who knows his guitar. When you have practiced your song to where you have some degree of loving understanding of your song—and when you have practiced your guitar chords (adding any little interspersals you choose to design as decor) till you feel they are a genuine help rather than a hindrance to your singing, the result when presented to a crowded house may fail to bring tumults of applause but it will not bring you into contumely, contempt, and bad repute.

The foregoing is as far as deponent chooseth to affirm and declare at this time. Possibly we could write a little book on the singer and his personally conducted guitar accompaniment. Possibly the book when published would go to a wide array of guitar players who strum their own accompaniments to their own vocal and verbal performances. It might help. And then again maybe not. In my earliest days, ending a program of readings with a group of songs to guitar accompaniment, I was able to hurdle one obstacle by a frank and simple statement. The audience appreciated being told that if every last one of them walked out of the hall and left me alone on the platform and the janitor turned out the lights, I would only be doing what I often did at home, sitting in a quiet dark corner and singing a few songs that I regard as nice or significant and perhaps priceless.

The time may come when there will be available an Anthology of the Guitar in Literature. As an instance, the Ecuador poet Jorge Carrera Andrade would be represented by various lines and passages from his noble book, Secret Country *(published by MacMillan's). Muna Lee translates:*

My mother, clothed in the setting sun,
put away her youth in a deep guitar,
and only on certain evenings would she show it to her children,
sheathed in music, light, and words.

Here, now, I pause in puzzlement over what could not conceivably be explained as a simple oversight in the chronicles of Sandburg's life, particularly in the obituaries: Sandburg was a national poet-hero who early began to make the guitar a central part of his life. Yet that aspect of his life is seldom mentioned. I speak here of the classic guitar—the guitar of Segovia—not, of course, the serviceable folk guitar Sandburg toted with him on tours, from which he coaxed his simple unrefined chords, to accompany his own beautiful homely singing. His frustration at being unable to draw from the guitar the beautiful sound he loved to hear was a blessing in disguise, however. He turned his frustrated fingers to another form of homage—a far, far better way of paying homage to the instrument—writing his poetry and prose.

We handed "The Definitions" over to our artist George Giusti, who fitted the words, which have become classic, into a classic shape.

Sandburg was a writer; myself, an artist. I did not know his craft, nor he mine. Our common ground was the guitar. That was how and where we met—on that vast playground, with plenty of room to romp around. Now Carl was a contributor to *The Guitar Review* and I was nominally his editor. We had to meet in his area. To my amazement, Carl took this relationship seriously. He actually expected me—yea, invited me—to lay my heavy blue pencil on his work, to edit the words of Carl Sandburg, poet laureate of America.

"I know you to be a man of taste and discrimination, not to mention intelligence and wit," he wrote me with "Definitions" and "Confession." "Therefore you are hereby authorized to make any kind of a goldarn shift or shuffle that seems to you right." Well, I shifted not, nor shuffled. In sheer unworthiness I shrank from touching even a goldarn serif of each sacred word.

As I knew him, Carl was always trying mischievously to extract the whimsical or comic from events or people that came his way. And he didn't have to try hard; invariably, he came up with something. Once it was the classic guitar and its distinguished master, Andrés Segovia.

In early spring 1955, we received such a piece from Sandburg, written expressly for "our magazine." It was short and simply entitled "Subway Conversation." In colloquial lingo, unseemly when placed in juxtaposition with the genteel classic guitar, two guys riding the subway are having a discussion, if not an argument. They are speaking of Andrés Segovia, the world's greatest master of the classic guitar, as they might of a ball player or a prize fighter; about Segovia, the champion of the instrument, protector of its purity and innocence, and an implacable warrior against any vulgarization of it. Carl knew this for as long as he'd known Segovia—almost twenty years—and in view of this he had some misgivings about how his "Subway Conversation" would be received. He wrote me:

A chattel with a soul often in part owning its owner, and tantalizing him with his lack of perfection & an instrument of quaint form and quiet demeanor dedicated to the dulcet rather than the diapason & a box of chosen wood having intimate accessories wherefrom sound may be measured and commanded to the interest of ears not lost to hammer crash or wind whisper—A portable companion distinguished from the piano in that you can take it with you neither horses nor motor truck being involved & a small friend weighing less than a newborn infant, ever responsive to all sincere efforts aimed at mutual respect, depths of affection or love gone off the deep end & a device in the realm of harmonic creation where six silent strings have the sound potential of profound contemplation or happy go lucky whim & a highly evolved contrivance whereby delicate melodic moments mingle with punctuation of silence bringing "the creative hush" & a vibratory implement under incessant practice and skilled cajolery giving out with serene maroon meditations. Flame dancers in scarlet sashes. snow white acrobats plunging into black mid night pools, odd numbers in evening green waltzing with even numbers in dawn pink

The Guitar, some definitions as felt by Carl Sandburg

The enclosed may be suitable for our magazine, The Guitar Review. *And again it may not be. And in the matter of what is fun, funny, and in good taste, I would as soon trust you as anyone in the United States or Mexico. If it would bother Segovia in the slightest way, I would not want to print it. As I go on playing his recordings, he continues to grow in the marvels of technique and in moving shadows and colors of the human spirit. And my salutations to you for the way you keep faith with the guitar and make it bring ever new meanings.*

Ever yours,

Carl

I acknowledged his letter, thanked him for the manuscript, and suggested that I prepare some drawings to illustrate the piece. Sandburg answered June 23, 1955, as follows:

June 23, 1955

Dear Greg:

Yes—illustrations, drawings by you will fix up my piece "Subway Conversation," force people to take it as funny with no hidden ironic intents . . . I thank you for the drawing; I shall treasure it. And a handwritten letter from you could not be thrown away. . . . I was going to step in and have you write some letters for me because my spelling is so poor and my grammar are which not could be . . . But I will tell you sometime that when I count the 100 richest men in America I include you . . . Of course, "Subway Conversation" was written EXPRESSLY FOR THE GOOD OLD GUITAR REVIEW.

Your ever-loving,

Carl

It must be noted here that even as recently as 1955, as musical history goes, the classic guitar was mainly appreciated by the old aficionados of the thirties and forties. It later came to wide acceptance as a serious instrument. Virgil Thompson wrote, "There is only one guitar, and that is the Classic Guitar, and Andrés Segovia is its prophet." Both instrument and man were sacrosanct. Levity about either could lead to banishment from the order. Had not the Maestro almost fifty years before taken the guitar out of the smoky taverns of Spain into the clear cultured air of the concert halls of the world's capitals?

Thus, a rather stuffy seriousness pervaded the guitar scene; nobody made jokes about it. Although Segovia is a man of great humor and himself possesses a rare gift for storytelling, especially in the light ironic vein, an allegory such as Carl's "Subway Conversation" in which Segovia's gentle art is placed in comradeship with the crude craft of fisticuffs might cause consternation, perhaps not to the Maestro, as Carl feared, but certainly to his worshippers—our pristine readers.

But I am sure Andrés would have loved the piece. Though Segovia and I shared the common ground of the guitar, we also shared the telling of funny stories. Whenever we met, we always had some good ones for each other.

Yes, I believe Andrés would have loved this piece so endearingly written for him by his old friend and former "pupil" Carl Sandburg. But we cautious editors could not take a chance, and especially timorous was our chief, the fastidiously conservative Bobri. As for showing it at all to Segovia for the decision that would remove all doubt, there never was an opportunity. We could never pin him down when he was in town. In those days he was quickly in and out. Finally, after much discussion about it, we filed it and forgot it, as many editors would do. I preserved Carl's signed original manuscript, of course. And Carl forgot it, too. At least, he never mentioned it or missed it in subsequent issues.

SUBWAY CONVERSATION

"There is only one Segovia."

"Sure, sure, how could there be more than one Segovia?"

"Well, what I mean is if there was more than one Segovia you would hear about it."

"I know what you mean, you're trying to say nobody has yet come along who can stand up to Segovia and trade punches and come out even."

"You talk like Segovia is a prize fighter, a leather pusher."

"Well, a champeen is a champeen, ain't he?"

"Sure and an artist is an artist."

"And if an artist has what it takes and has won more fights than any others in the field, why can't I say he's a champeen?"

"All right, have it your way but I come right back to what I started with."

"And what was that?"

"I said there is only one Segovia and you got smart and had to ask me how could there be more than one Segovia."

"Well, by cracky, I'm comin' back again to ask you how could there be two Segovias."

"And the last time you said that, I told you, of course if there was more than one Segovia we would hear about it."

"Sure, sure, and since we don't hear there's two Segovias of course there's only one."

"And that's what I started to tell you and you wanted an argument—here's my station now and I'm getting off and my last word to you is the same as my first—there is only one Segovia."

Like Segovia, Carl Sandburg was no mere static name heavily embossed on a costly letterhead of parchmentlike paper. For a time Carl Sandburg actually worked for us. But in those years—the mid-fifties—he had reached the pinnacle of his fame: television wanted him, Hollywood wanted him, magazine and newspaper interviewers wanted him, the concert stage wanted him. We wanted him—but we were his leisure, his rest, his relaxation—and there was little time for that. "Subway Conversation," though never printed, was his last offering to *The Guitar Review.*

Carl never ceased to be a keen reader and a frequent visitor to New York, however. Often he sent us postcards. Once he even phoned from Connemara, his home in Flat Rock, North Carolina. "Where's the *Review?*" he asked.

In 1959, we reprinted his "Guitar Definitions," in another format this time, with my drawing of him. Like a fledgling writer who'd just broken into print, he awaited the appearance of that issue with great eagerness. It was our first issue on "The Guitar in the United States," and when at last it was out, a few copies were specially mailed to him. We immediately got a check with a request for ten or more copies of the same, and a humble inquiry as to the availability of the original of my drawing which accompanied the piece. I sent it to him like a shot, and it hangs now in the Carl Sandburg birthplace in Galesburg, Illinois. In 1960, the drawing was borrowed for use in Harry Golden's *Carl Sandburg.*

Carl Sandburg said it was an old family custom to die at an age divisible by eleven. Sometime in his life when birthdays began to wear out their welcome—perhaps when he was sixty-six, when inexorable time had to be faced, and at least an armed truce made, he shot for seventy-seven in the corner pocket and made it, then for eighty-eight and again made it—just. But so far as I know, and despite the fun he had with that whimsical contest with Father Time, only his landmark birthdays were publicly celebrated—the seventy-fifth and the eightieth. On those noteworthy birthdays, the newspeople cornered him for interviews, and for several days, it was Carl Sandburg Birthday Time over all the land.

On January 6, 1953, he arrived at his seventy-fifth. On the same day his newest book, *Always the Young Strangers,* made a simultaneous appearance. A huge dinner celebrating both events was held at Chicago's Blackstone Hotel. Publishing figures, editors, writers, readers, and friends in other walks of life were there; all except his *Guitar Review* contingent. None of us was invited.

However, we got off a telegram to him. It was the least we could do, but it could not simply be the usual stereotype of the congratulatory wire—not to Carl, who never in his life resorted to such easy measures, if he knew they existed at all. No, our message had to be original and funny! So, reaching into what must have been the softest part of my brain, I plucked out this message:

Always, the Young Twangers—your New York Guitar Friends—think of you; especially on this wonderful day of your seventy-fifth birthday.

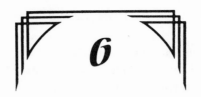

6

The Poet
Does His Duty

As the poet of the people, Carl Sandburg became the hungry but happy hunter of folk songs. These were the songs he itched to sing. They could hardly be called "poetry" in its lofty sense, but they said, by other routes, what his poetry says. They were songs of ethnic groups within the melting pot of early twentieth-century America, songs of regional differences, of customs, lingo, workmen, slogans, and love.

It was here in the anonymous folk song that Sandburg found satisfaction and pleasure when he needed to sing. The urgency was not that of personal catharsis, passing hangup, subjective distemper, or political harangue; it was a need to know America better and better through its songs and to give the songs voice lest they be forgotten. He was a rememberer and resurrector, doing a job of keeping intact and preserving the tenuous lines of the past.

If we must assign one single factor for the phenomenal rise of the guitar throughout the world over the past forty years, we need not look farther than the surge of interest in folk singing stirred by the great professionals who appeared in the late forties. For their bible, these singers of America and its roots went to the First Testament, the Gospel of the Folk Song according to Carl Sandburg: *The American Songbag,* published in 1926 by Harcourt Brace. Carl never presumptuously wrapped himself in the cloak of the expert, but throughout the laborious project he was a patient roundup man. He found the folk who had found the songs and knew their origins, though he himself had discovered many on his own. For years he had been waiting for some specialist to gather a bunch of songs between the covers of a book, so that when needed, they could be found at once. Sandburg had always felt such a need himself. His *Lincoln, Rootabaga Stories,* and now *The American Songbag* were written because he got tired of waiting for somebody else to write them. "Ain't it hell the way a book walks up to you and makes you write it?" he asked in a letter to fellow poet Amy Lowell in 1925 while deep in his *Prairie Years.*

Thus, after years of waiting to be written, *The American Songbag* finally bagged Sandburg, the logical candidate for the job. After all, his cry for getting the songs in one place had been the loudest and loneliest, and now he was resigned and willing to work for it. With the same energy and zeal that had seen him through *The Prairie Years,* he threw himself into the project.

The task, Sanburg soon realized, became more than mere rounding up of known and obscure folk songs. Over a hundred of the songs out of a total of 280 had never before been published. Carl then had to exert his authority as selector and editor to write introductory pieces for each song finally chosen from the many more hundreds that poured in. Were it a pure Carl Sandburg creation—words and music by him—with no responsibility for making selective judgments, the job would have been simpler. As it was, "[the job] has mounted beyond all first plans for it," he wrote to fellow poet Vachel Lindsay a few months before the *Songbag* finally came out. "It is not so much my book as that of a thousand other people who have made its 280 colonial, pioneer, railroad, work-gang, hobo, Irish, Negro, Mexican, gutter, gossamer songs, chants, and ditties."

"What are Mexican songs ('La Cucaracha,' 'Cielito Lindo,' 'Mananitas,' 'Lo Que Digo,' 'El Abandonado,' 'Adelita,' and 'Versos de Montalgo') doing in *The American Songbag?*" I asked Carl one day. It was a thoughtless question, I was soon embarrassed to admit.

"Mexico is in North America like the U.S. is," he answered, and then added, "and more people in Kalamazoo, Michigan, know 'Cielito Lindo' and 'La Cucaracha' than they do 'The Colorado Trail' or the 'Erie Canal.'"

But one song without such rationale found its way into *The*

Songbag anyway. This was "The John B. Sails," brought over from the Bahamian island of Nassau in the early twenties. It was discovered by Carl's great friends, *Chicago Tribune* cartoonist John T. McCutcheon and his wife. The song—a rueful tale about the comic calamities attending a sailing of the sloop John B. from Governor's Harbor, Nassau—was, in fact, authentic calypso. I don't think that its exotic origin and special rhythm impressed Carl too much. When I heard him sing it one boxcar evening in 1950, I never suspected that buried under the Carl Sandburg free delivery style lay even a suggestion of the calypso idiom. He sang the song with his customary gusto and fervor, as he sang all songs, in a tempo abounding in his own *rubato*. When a song was over, there were always a few beats lying around that he'd stolen from one measure and had forgotten to pay back to succeeding ones. Of course, he employed his serviceable all-purpose three-chord accompaniment. The characteristics of calypso, which had by then taken great hold here and were instantly recognizable whenever heard, were not exactly evoked by Sandburg whenever he tackled "The John B. Sails." But like all songs he ever ventured to sing, he made it sound so much his own that when later I heard sophisticated groups sing it—The Weavers, The Beachboys—it was the Sandburg version that I always preferred.

Although Carl Sandburg's instrument of accompaniment had been the guitar since 1906, there isn't a note of guitar music, even a mention of the instrument in *The American Songbag*. Each song was arranged with a piano setting, very professional and quite sophisticated—even to the use of flowery Italian musical directions. I cannot help but smile when I see, for example, *allegretto giocoso* suggesting the mood for a slangy circus song called "Si Hubbard." The arrangements in *Songbag* were evidently meant to be something more than mere scratchings on a guitar. These were the mid-twenties; good instruments and good players were yet decades away.

The piano was still very much the queen of the parlor. At parties, squatting there royally, she received the homage of guests gathered about her for the inevitable sing of the evening. *The American Songbag* was on many a piano music rack in those days.

In 1950, *The New American Songbag* was published. Beginning with a foreword by Bing Crosby in appreciation of Sandburg's search for long-lost songs, the book includes not only favorites from *The American Songbag,* but also many new ones that Carl had since discovered in his constant quest for songs. During those years the guitar had begun its ascendancy and by 1950 was firmly established. Thus the guitar was woven into the new arrangements of *The New American Songbag* in the form of chord symbols. Now any would-be folk singer, however musically illiterate, could accompany any song in the book by simply reading the chord symbols over the words. Thus, a nation of adolescents, at the acne of their perfection, could drag out their guitars, finger the three or four simple chords provided, and croak away about the time when they were bachelors, living by themselves, working at the weaver's trade and keeping fair young maids from the foggy, foggy dew.

Like a sun-crazed, sand-worn prospector seeks gold, Carl Sandburg hunted for songs. But he didn't selfishly poach them. After discovering a lode lying dormant and unsung, he quickly shared his find with others; and soon a newly unearthed song was on everyone's lips—and on many a professional's program.

"A new song learnt is worth more to me than any Japanese print or rare painting. I can take it into a railroad train or a jail or anywheres," Sandburg wrote to his fellow song-seeker Isadora Bennett Reed in 1921. "Go on picking up songs," he urged his poet friend Jacob Zeitlin in a 1925 letter. "You'll never be searched for them; they'll never get you into trouble."

The concept of a large collection of songs in one volume was a Sandburg aim from the time he began troubadouring across the country in 1916 and gathering songs en route. The actual work involved in producing *The American Songbag* took several years. By 1925 when the work had the go-ahead of publisher Alfred Harcourt, Sandburg had not only discovered many songs on his own, but many "owners" of songs. By May 1927, he'd rounded up some 340 songs which originally were intended to make up a two-volume *Songbag,* but it was deemed more practical to have one large volume than two smaller ones. By judicious pruning, Carl finally settled for one 280-song volume. Until just a few weeks before publication date, Sandburg was busy making revisions, additions, and elisions, even crossing the musical editorial line over into the art department to experiment with the decorative scrolls on the cover layout. He was sure the dummy was perfect. "It gives an immediate impression," he wrote to Harcourt Brace designer Howard Clark in September 1927, "that it will stand wear, stand on pianos, stand punishment, stand throwing at cats or dogs." But it was the cover that gave Sandburg concern: he was afraid that it would not do right by the inside of the book, and several designs were tried before one pleased him entirely.

It was a difficult job of bookmaking. To this one, as with no other book he undertook, he was father, mother, and midwife. He was glad when all loose ends were finally tied up. But his humor had never deserted him, and toward the end of his labors he sent an appropriate sign-off message in his usual alliterative, playful wording to Hazel Felman Buchbinder: "We're on the last pizza-cato pinnacles of the peaks."

In early November 1927, *The Songbag* behind him, Carl wrote to H. L. Mencken of his great relief at the completion of the task. For a number of weeks between the time he'd checked the last note and word of the book and its appearance that winter, he shamelessly loafed. "I am the laziest man in the United States," he wrote his friend, whom he called Hank. "The detail work (on the book) nearly killed me."

Though Sandburg was the first to admit that the book was unfinished and that many, many more songs were tucked away in corners of the world waiting to be unearthed, he was glad to have at least scratched the surface. As he wrote H. L. Mencken again a few months later, "My gratification about the book is merely that of a patriot who has seen his duty and done it."

7

The Poet Performs

THE HOBO RUGGEDNESS and aw-shucks simplicity of Carl Sandburg were hardly the characteristics you would expect to find in one so completely fascinated by the finely rarefied, delicately evanescent sound of the Spanish guitar. But Carl was first a poet—and when he first heard the guitar played by the master Segovia, he was hooked for the rest of his life. He drifted to it, followed it eagerly, sought it out wherever he was. When he knew that guitar people were within phoning and taxi distance, he would soon join the heady company of guitarists, a shawl over his knee, drinking from a beaker of bourbon in short sips, drinking in the music in long draughts.

An instrument of poetry, Carl sang his praise to this most poetic of instruments.

He was the guitar's great poet-champion; but as a professional who used the instrument in his work, he was its least player. *Least* player, I said, not worst; for while there are scores who play much more guitar than Sandburg ever could, there are many unfeeling Philistines who, for all their flashy guitar work, cheapen and vulgarize the instrument.

Sandburg's reverence for the guitar could not have been shown more convincingly than in the way he played it—gently, shyly—like a bashful swain mooning over a maid above his station.

He was not a poor player; he was simply an unplayer. Never have I known a singer to employ so minimally a guitar background to his songs and yet to achieve so maximally a pleasing, just-right-result.

It has been said that Carl Sandburg the guitarist was a one-chord man—or, more generously, a two-chord man, and sometimes, in great charity, even as much as a three-chord man, and that the frets beyond the first position of the guitar were *terra incognita* to him.

In truth, his repertoire of chords was actually more in the neighborhood of ten. However, all of them were basic, uncut by sixths or ninths or other nuances of harmony.

These comments on Carl Sandburg's guitar playing usually come with curl of lip, as the speaker looks down his narrow, aristocratic nose at the primitive, nonclassic approach to the guitar of a singer like Sandburg. Among these purists, none was more rigid or vigilant of the sanctity of our instrument than I, even if the blasphemer was my beloved friend Sandburg. But frequent contact with Carl and knowledge of his warmth, his sincerity, as well as his unpretentiousness and simplicity, soon made me a completely captivated disciple. Which is what everybody else became, sooner or later.

When Sandburg was on, the playing was *not* the thing.

Years ago, just before World War II, a noted ballade singer, Frank Schildt of Holland, guitarist, linguist, musician, and sophisticate, then in Paris, by chance heard a recording of Carl Sandburg. It stopped him short.

"It grabbed me," said Schildt. Not only had he never heard Carl Sandburg, he'd never heard *of* him. "First of all," he continued, "the voice was untrained, even primitive; he lost measure after measure, and his guitar accompaniment, what there was of it, was shot through with doubtful chords. But it grabbed me." He could not accept Sandburg as even basically accurate musically, but the poetic conviction, even on a depersonalized disk, got through to Schildt.

Most of the songs Carl sang were simple, three-or-four chord pieces of music, during which he did not wander from the simple track of the harmony. For a song like "Jimmy Crack Corn," Carl's ear was good enough to take him to the correct places on the fingerboard of the guitar. But one song he often attempted was "September Song" by Kurt Weill. This is a piece with fine musical color and subtle harmony. The guitar accompaniment takes some study and no little technical skill, especially for such rueful lyrics as Maxwell Anderson wrote for "September Song." Yet Carl, with only the sketchiest idea of what the accompaniment should be, sang the song on a CBS radio broadcast on his seventy-ninth birthday in 1957. His playing was effortless and smooth, though unfortunately incorrect most of the time. He hit only the higher peaks of the harmonic demands made by the song. On the other hand, his guitar was unobtrusive, spare, and at times hardly audible, which was probably all to the good. So again, guitar shortcomings notwithstanding, Sandburg put the song over by the sheer power of his self-confidence, of his certainty that this was a song for him to sing, and that he could sing it right. And he did.

"September Song" was a number Carl and I did together often. It was part of what we jokingly called "our act" at parties. I had learned the accurate accompaniment to it from the sheet music itself, adding a few embellishments of my own, and though Carl had no thought ever of accommodating his "version" to mine, he nevertheless enjoyed singing the song with "d'Alezzzzioh at the guitar," as he so grandly introduced me when we were doing the party circuit.

At the time of his CBS birthday broadcast, he was our house guest at Henderson Place and the taping was actually done in our living room the day before the broadcast. "September Song" was one of several to be interspersed throughout the program, and Carl saw his opportunity to get a guitar pal on the air with him. He collared Joe Wershba, producer of the show, and made him set up the tape recorder before us. After a few takes, we had a pretty good recording of the song in the can. Though a little nervous, I had managed to do most of what I felt should be done on the guitar, and Carl beamed at me proudly during the playback. Shortly after that, the Missus and I had to get off to an evening appointment, leaving Carl, Joe, and the rest of the CBS crew to continue the taping. The next night, I exulted, I would be on the air! In the company of Carl Sandburg! As his guitar accompanist, doing a great song together!

But our collaboration never got out of the can. To be sure, as scheduled, the song was on the program the next night, but it was Carl alone, doing his own guitar accompaniment. My dream of overnight fame was dashed.

After Terry and I left for our date the evening before, Joe Wershba pondered the out-of-character sophistication of my guitar as juxtaposed to the famous trademark simplicity of Sandburg's voice. He decided to retape the song, this time with Carl's own wandering but providentially faint and cloudy guitar background. It may have been musically incorrect, but it was warm, safe, simple, and comfortable—as long as it was all Sandburg.

In Carl's meagerly filled chord-bag, there was one that he always pulled out when in doubt—and its structure was so abstract, so vague and imprecise, that it fitted into any juncture of the harmonic progression of a song. When he was not sure whether it was time for the tonic, or subdominant or dominant, like a flash, the gnarled index and middle fingers of his left hand ran out into left field and brought in the chord. It was formed at the fifth fret of the first string and the fourth fret of the second string, and plucked gently with the index and middle fingers of the right hand. Its quality was something between a diminished and an augmented chord, and it seemed to serve anywhere at any time.

The stories of Sandburg's shortcomings as a guitarist were not long in reaching his ears, but they troubled him not at all. "I'll never be Segovia, that's for sure," he chuckled one day as he plucked his simplistic chords between his words, "and if I can't get to be that good, I'd rather be what I am."

To Sandburg, the song was the thing; this was what people paid to hear. A harmonic slip here and there along the path of a song never detracted from its impact. Even a departure from the proper tuning of his instrument was no calamity. Sometimes, in the course of a concert, the strings of the guitar, though having been put in proper tune at the start, slowly, almost imperceptibly slipped from their moorings as most are wont to do, and drifted off sourly.

After such a development one evening in New York, a brilliant young guitarist known for his severity and uncompromising perfectionism approached Sandburg backstage, and, barely concealing his snobbery behind a studied casualness, remarked: "I enjoyed the concert very much, sir, but I thought I should tell you that your guitar was out of tune all during the second half of the program."

"Oh, was it?" said Carl in mock surprise. "Well, I'm sure only a great musician like yourself noticed it."

Inevitably, as it has been with poets from Chaucer to Shakespeare, from Burns to Whitman, composers have also been moved by Sandburg's poems to write musical settings for them. Years before, Maestro Segovia wrote out a scale for him to practice, but Carl never did locate that first note of the guitar diapason. Now and then, at a party, he would sing a satirically funny ditty, usually an extemporaneous outburst on a contemporary theme. Its melody was always so simple and so derivative as to be actually the music of another song.

Carl did not perform musical settings of his own works, but stayed in the warm, familiar company of "Frankie and Johnny," "Barbara Allen," "Kitty," "The Lonesome Cowboy," and other comfortable old friends who were around long before he began his own contributions to American culture with *Chicago Poems, Cornhuskers, Smoke and Steel,* and *The People, Yes.*

He kept singing the handed-down folk songs until he could no longer lift guitar or voice. Like a grandfather's old watch which belonged to his father before him, or a Bible with a pressed rose in its pages, the songs were precious heirlooms changing custodianship with each generation. Carl's pleasure was more than the mere act of singing them; it was doubled if an adventure or an interesting story was built up in the course of his eventual excavation of a song—and the more tortuous the path, the greater satisfaction and zest he put into his singing of it.

Most folk songs go on interminably, especially the narrative variety, those that begin with "Come listen to my story." I have always been grateful to Carl for never having sung, in my presence anyway, a song of more than three verses. I think that I may have been really won over when he made his first offering of a quatrain in which the melodrama of life and death is offered in only *fourteen* words. It goes like this, to a basic blues melody:

> *Papa loved mama*
> *Mama loved men*
> *Mama's in the graveyard*
> *Papa's in the pen.*

Another shorty that Carl liked to sing whenever its theme, a political one, seemed apropos, was one of his own compositions—whipped up during the full flush of his involvement in the 1940 campaign when Wendell Willkie opposed FDR for the presidency of the United States. A fervent supporter of FDR and the New Deal, Sandburg saw Willkie as a reactionary and a tool of Wall Street—in short, an emissary of the continued power of the Depression-era Establishment.

The words of Carl's song were set to the tune of "God Bless America," which Kate Smith was singing all over the air waves in the early forties. But the words of Sandburg's concoction, alas, were not a benediction, exactly; they were, in fact, an imprecation of withering scorn and condemnation. They went:

> *Goddam Republicans*
> *Scum of the earth*
> *We will meet them*
> *And beat them*
> *And show them what we are worth.*
> *Out of Wall Street,*
> *Came a Willkie*
> *He's a silkie*
> *S. O. B.*
> *Goddam Republicans*
> *The G-e-e-e O-h-h-h P-e-e-e!*

I first heard the G.O.P. song in 1952 out of the blue one night at a party at Henderson Place. Carl Sandburg suddenly picked up a guitar, threw his head back, and boomed it out. At first it seemed extemporaneous, since 1952 was an election year, and we were in the midst of the Eisenhower-Stevenson campaign for the presidency. Obviously, when the name Willkie cropped up, the anachronism placed the song at a time some twelve years before. Carl's hero then was FDR; his hero in 1952 was Adlai Stevenson, whom he idolized with the feelings returned in good measure. In fact, there was talk during the Democratic convention in Chicago that Carl Sandburg's name would be placed in nomination as running mate with his fellow Illinoisan, Adlai Stevenson.

But Sandburg's target was actually the GOP, not well-meaning, One Worlder Willkie, dead since 1944, who'd long been regenerated and redeemed, exonerated and purged of all preelection sins, even by Carl.

The song was just one of many that Sandburg could conceive on the spot. There was the ballad he sang one evening in 1951 shortly after the death of his one-time employer, William Randolph Hearst. Sandburg had worked for Hearst briefly but disapproved of him, calling him mountebank and monster. The commemorative ballad Sandburg sang to us that evening was sad and touching, even compassionate. At this point, I should produce the words, but I cannot. Carl sang them only once in our presence, and nobody took them down, nor did he himself remember them afterward, I'll wager. Anyway, one phrase, one passing ironical comment was repeated after each stanza as a kind of *l'envoi*, whose words I'm sure I can recall:

William Randolph Hearst lived in a house with a thousand rooms
But he could only die in one of them.

In 1921, Sandburg wrote a letter to fellow poet Witter Bynner, concerning financial terms of a coming booking before a chapter of the Poetry Society of America which Bynner had been trying to arrange if Carl could fit it into his schedule. Carl said in part and in some asperity, "I am a hoofer and a writer and would rather loaf and write, and pick up a guitar with the proper vags, than to deliver spoken exhortations before any honorable bodies wheresoever."

Carl Sandburg, newspaperman, poet, and all-round journeyman writer, began in 1916 to branch out into a supplementary career—that of lecturer on diverse subjects, and reader of verse, undiverse: his own. Along with his books, notes, scripts, and other papers that make up the paraphernalia of the public platform performer, Carl toted a battered steel-stringed guitar and, dragging it out after his lecture, announced almost apologetically that the few folk songs he would sing tied in with the folk quality he tried always to get into his verse. "They are all authentic songs people have sung for years," Sandburg explained. "If you don't care for them and want to leave the hall, it will be all right with me. I'll only be doing what I'd be doing at home, all by myself, anyway."

In fact, the songs which constituted the tail end of the main body of his programs in the early days quickly became the tail that wagged the dog. Not only did the customers stay for the songs, they seemed to like them even better than the poetry. "Bring your guitar," was the insistent rejoinder to every invitation or booking.

Performing became his second, but by no means lesser, profession.

Sandburg seldom missed an opportunity to quote the seventeenth-century French scientist-philosopher Blaise Pascal on solitude: "The miseries of men come from not being able to sit alone in a quiet room." Carl Sandburg's amen to that might well have included a postscript: "with a guitar."

Sandburg liked to sit with a guitar in his room at home, surrounded by his papers, letters, pens, pencils, typewriter, hats, coats, books, shawls, scarfs, favorite chairs and favorite pictures, old and new; a finger or two of bourbon; a green, scuffed, city desk visor; old cheroots, smoked down to inch-size. In other parts of the large, hushed house, his beloved family slept safe, warm, comfortable; and beyond his room lay the world as calm as he could help make it that day.

It is an irony that before he could fulfill the dream of sanctuary from the outside world in the "quiet room," he had to plunge into the outside world itself in order to underwrite that dream. Well before radio and television, he was already a public figure. Though the vagabond poet's spirit was strong within him, he was not irresponsible; where his family was concerned, he was a paragon of rectitude and conscience. Before he would even indulge himself with a stump of a cigar, he would first see to the needs and the welfare of Paula and his growing family.

Thus, with his guitar and verses, he went on long barnstorming tours to earn the money that would buy comfort for his family and hours of solitude for soul-searching and the pressing need to write as he was born to do.

In the "quiet room," lifting his voice in song at least once a day was good for his soul tone, just as lifting a chair over his head once a day was good for his muscle tone. His singing was a ritual, a prayer, an act of faith. His tones came out earnestly, with almost religious insistency, just on the outside chance that by some cosmic fluke, nobody in the world happened to want to sing that day or simply forgot to. So here was faithful Carl, when he felt "at all in health," dutifully picking up his guitar and seeing to it that at least one song was in the air.

His dynamics lay not in tone production, but in his sense of the drama, message, or character of a song. He saw no need ever to accommodate his voice output to the size of a hall; rather he let it become clear at the very outset of a concert that the audience would have to accommodate itself to him, simply by sitting quietly and listening attentively. Sandburg's voice might be soft, even sweet, but it was penetrating and could find its way into every hidden recess of the hall, no matter what its capacity. When the electronic age arrived, many a microphone was shoved before the singer by anxious stagehands. Carl did not refuse them, but he didn't make too strenuous a point of using them, either. With quiet amusement, he seemed to tolerate the device as a gadget without whose help he'd gotten along fine for over forty years and could for many more.

His voice, technically, was in the baritone range; so say the musicians. But the component parts that made up its unique quality were his real American sound—simple, perhaps, but mature, authentic, vibrant with a lyric lilt, and intuitive feeling.

Lloyd Lewis, his old friend and co-singer in many a boxcar night in Chicago, wrote in 1925: "Sandburg may not be a great singer, but his singing is great."

Sandburg knew his way around an audience. His stage presence was less presence than homey visit; it was ingenuous and offhand, and it worked. He had developed a shrewd sense of audience reaction; he knew its predilections, caprices, and enthusiasms. Indeed, he was even confident enough to advise Isadora Bennett Reed, who'd sent him some songs she'd discovered in January 1921: "If you are ever changing your line of work, and going on stage with an act, better let me give you my hunches on how to use these songs. It's been amazing to me to see how audiences rise to 'em; how the lowbrows just naturally like 'Frankie an' Johnny,' while the highbrows, with the explanation that the murder and adultery is less in percentage than in the average grand opera, love 'em, too!"

His bag of songs and his guitar were, like his trusty long johns, a part of his duffle and next to his skin wherever he went. He was a troubadour, undaunted and uninhibited. "On some trip to New York," he wrote to Helen Keller in October 1929, "I shall phone and ask whether I can come out and bring my guitar and songs." In 1938, he told Franklin D. Roosevelt in a letter to "expect me someday at the White House door with a guitar, for an evening of songs and of stories from the hinterlands which may rest you on one hell of a job."

But no anecdote, note in history, or memoir shows that Sandburg ever got around to ringing the White House doorbell anyway. He was as busy in his way as the president, deep in the last agonizing chapters of his four-volume *Abraham Lincoln: The War Years*.

On a balmy May evening in the early fifties, Carl Sandburg walked through our wide-open door. In town for only a few days, he immediately suggested that we organize a party for later that evening.

He gave us some names and phone numbers of friends he particularly wanted to see, and we added a few of our own. As always, the list of guests grew and grew. I knew that Carl would not complain of a large party; indeed, he liked big shindigs. As long as he had his armchair, cheroots, scarves, shawls, a bourbon at hand, and a guitar in his lap, he could have had a good time on the Bronx express during rush hour.

"Let 'em come, let 'em come," he said. "Better to risk a stampede of too many than risk a slight to even one."

Henderson Place was quiet and peaceful in the dusk of evening. The poplar trees, somewhat oversized for so small a street, had begun to bud fragrantly, and even the last good-night chirpings of the raspy sparrows in the eaves sounded sweetly melancholic.

The party had been called for seven o'clock. About an hour before, Sandburg descended the stairs to take his accustomed place in the party room. He looked fresh and healthy. He'd changed to a new shirt, and its whiteness competed with the whiteness of his hair. All was in readiness for the party. He sat in the armchair and adjusted the scarves and shawls which Terry brought him. A fifth of Jack Daniels and a glass were at his elbow. My Augustine guitar was nearby, lying in its open case. Carl gestured toward it, and I brought it over. Then I went upstairs to dress, and the Missus went downstairs to the kitchen to finish her food-fixing before she, too, dressed for the party.

Now Carl was alone in the room, with a guitar. Behind him, a lamp glowed softly. Soon the deep sweet vibrations of his voice and the spare, gentle strains of his guitar began to well up in the house.

This was not his own house, not his own room, but in New York it was as close as he could come to home if open-armed welcome, warmth, and affection had anything to do with it.

I hurried down to join Carl, who'd never stopped singing. To my surprise, three guests sat on a sofa, and two others sat on the floor. They'd walked through the open door and taken their places silently. Carl kept playing without any pauses of greeting. He was in the middle of a ritual. Amenities would come later.

Voices and footsteps of new arrivals, not yet in range of Carl's voice, echoed along the quiet street—falling to a hush and tiptoe silence as they approached the open door.

So it went for more than half an hour, as the guests entered quietly, one by one, and found places where they remained, silent and motionless, all attention on Carl.

The Poet Performs

The last few lines of the final song lingered in the air. Carl the folk singer with his guitar faded into Carl the white-haired preacher coming to the end of a long scripture. He raised his head and looked about the room, surprised to see all the people gathered there—some sitting, some standing, some at his feet.

Then he gave a grinning invocation, and the party began.

8

Boxes of
Chosen Woods

THE BANJO IS TO MUSICAL INSTRUMENTS what bourbon is to alcoholic liquors: both are 100 percent indigenously American, and Carl Sandburg liked them both. They ranked high among the many pleasures of his long life.

It was the plunky, unsophisticated banjo that Carl played from his boyhood to his twenty-sixth year. Then he was exposed to the more exotic, versatile guitar, and he switched to it for all time. Callous dismissal, however, was never part of Sandburg's makeup. His old feeling for his banished banjo would surge up within him from time to time.

One evening late in 1949, Carl crossed over from his digs at C. D. Batchelor's apartment in Tudor City to ours next door for dinner. Soon we were seated in the living room strumming guitars and lugubriously harmonizing "Nellie Gray" and "Old Black Joe." We began talking of the stringed instruments—old and new, endemic and exotic—and how it was that only the banjo could be categorized as truly native, improvised by the first slaves, using the principle of the jungle drum and stretching strings across it.

"Up to about eight years ago," Carl said, "there was always a banjo kickin' around the house." And he added wistfully, "Yep, I kinda miss havin' one around."

For almost forty years, the banjo, neglected perhaps, but still loved and not entirely out of mind, had stood in some corner of the house Sandburg lived in; now it was gone forever.

Sandburg told the story: "Back in 1942," he said "we were living in Harbert [Michigan]. Earl Robinson was staying with us, and he got started on how he loved the old-time banjo. So I gave him mine. After all, I'd stopped using it twenty years before, when I gave it up for the guitar. But I do miss it kickin' around the house, anyway."

That was all Carl vouchsafed to me of the old banjo and his apparent regret at having so impulsively let it go. Now Carl reached for the guitar and growled out an old minstrel song more suited to the banjo of yesteryear than to his new-found guitar.

Not until the publication of *The Letters of Carl Sandburg* did I get the full story of the banjo giveaway. A letter to Norman Corwin dated March 24, 1941, tells it. Robinson and Corwin had created a one-act opera for radio, based on Sandburg's *The People, Yes*. Robinson visited the Sandburgs in Harbert one day, and during the "front-room luncheon of plain proletarian baked beans with a classy divertissement of goat's milk, Erll [as Sandburg liked to spell Robinson's first name] told me of being on the lookout for an old-time five-string banjo. So yrs truly reaches over, tipping back his chair, into a corner behind two guitars and a Filipino three-string fiddle and produces a banjo tt [Sandburg's shorthand for "that"] yrs truly has had going on thirty yrs, not playing it for twenty years because a guitar had priority.

"It was like a good deacon," Sandburg's letter continued, "giving away an adopted child that had always been well-behaved to another good deacon who pledged to bring it up well-behaved and godly." Thus, the Sandburg home became banjoless. But Carl knew that in Robinson's charge, it would not only be more appreciated, it would also get played.

Even in 1927, over twenty years after Sandburg had switched from banjo to the guitar, there were still some insensitive listeners who couldn't tell the difference between the two instruments. Or they simply called *any* stringed instrument a banjo, or worse sometimes, even a *mandolin,* as Robert Frost did, in a letter to Sandburg back in the 1920s.

In covering Carl's early recitals, *Century Magazine* persistently referred to Carl's guitar as a banjo. Such sloppy reporting needed censure, and Carl got off a letter to the editor of the magazine. The letter is Sandburg at his drollest, and even then, he was beginning to rough out his famous definitions of the guitar which appeared in their final form in *The Guitar Review* twenty-two years later. The letter first came to my attention in 1948, when Carl thought it would amuse me, and sent me a copy of it.

To the Editor:

Would you kindly correct the statement published a number of times that in the song-offering in my recital concerts I employ a banjo?

The instrument used is one with less percussion and more intimations of silence than a banjo.

Sometimes when the strings of it are thrummed one has to listen twice to find the chord and the melody.

The box of the instrument is entirely of wood, with a cunning construction, having had centuries of study, rehearsal, and try-out by Italians, Spaniards, and the same Arabians who hunted up the Arabic numerals.

At music stores and pawnshops the instrument is called a Guitar.

The banjo is meant for jigs, buck and wing dances, attack, surprise, riot and rout. The guitar is intended for serenades, croons, for retreat, retirement, fadeaway.

I thank you.

Carl Sandburg

It was in April 1910 that Carl Sandburg, then married for two years, proudly announced the arrival of his first guitar.

Paula Sandburg was in Beaver Dam, Wisconsin, at the time. Carl was in Milwaukee, where he was struggling to nail down a job at Kroeger's Department Store writing advertising copy and counting the days until Paula could join him in the bungalow he had rented. The letter read in part ". . . now [we] have a guitar and there will be songs warbled and melodies whistled to the low Mexican humming of Paula-and-Cully's new stringed instrument." (Cully was Carl's boyhood nickname.) Thus, before he went on the road to sing for the masses, Carl Sandburg sang at home with the Missus.

Before his discovery of the classic Spanish model after World War II, Sandburg's early guitars were of solid American-make, heavy, steel-stringed, and robustly merry. He owned twin Washburn guitars, a pair of American beauties, pear-shaped of body but not pear-shaped of voice. Metallic strings do not make a beautiful tone. The early gut

It was on this day in April 1957 that Frank Lloyd Wright dubbed Carl Sandburg "Old Troubadour". Enjoying themselves in a suite at New York's elegant Plaza Hotel were (l. to r.) Sandburg, *Newsday* reporter Virginia Pasley, Wright, and Alicia Patterson Guggenheim, publisher of *Newsday*. (*Newsday* photo, provided to the author by V. Pasley.)

Carl and I were enjoying the guitar wizardry of Mirko Markovich one evening in 1950. (Photograph by Dr. John Richter, guitar by Albert Augustine.)

𝒯he first meeting of the mentor Andrès Segovia and his would-be pupil Carl Sandburg took place in the Chicago home of Dr. Jacob Robert and Mrs. Hazel Buchbinder on May 21, 1938. Once Segovia had tuned up the poet's Washburn guitar, Carl was off and singing. (Photo by Dr. Buchbinder.)

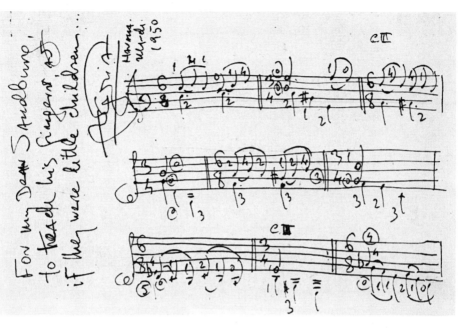

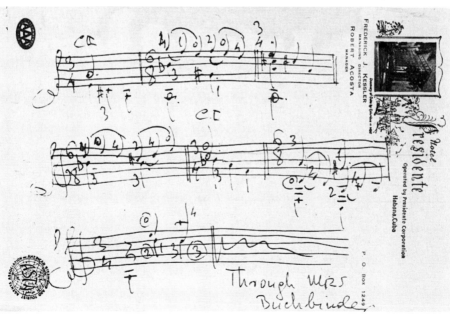

Sandburg's belated first lesson from maestro Segovia; given to Hazel Buchbinder at a Havana restaurant in 1950. The inscription reads: "For my dear Sandburg, to teach his fingers as if they were little children."

The mexican song — "Number 2" — which
Sandburg asked to hear me play on the guitar is on
next page
al dismo

Tres canciones populares mexicanas

Transcription de
ANDRÉS SEGOVIA

I

Manuel M. Ponce

32056

G. A. 111

The composition which Carl loved the most in my repertoire.
He would ask for it repeatedly; the enforced practice gave my
fingers their own tactile memory.

II

32056

Goddam the Republicans!
Scum of the earth...

Favorite
Sandburg song: to the tune of "God Bless America".

The words of Sandburg's own composition were not a benediction, but an imprecation of withering scorn, to the unlikely tune of "God Bless America".

𝄐 purchased this Martin guitar from Albert Augustine for $100 in 1947; after Sandburg and Segovia had played it I was loath to "wipe away the invisible finger traces of memory," even though my guitar pals questioned me about its dusty condition. The instrument was stolen one year later as I waited on a platform at Grand Central Station. Painting in background is one of my own, a view of the East River from Tudor City, Manhattan. (Photo by Dr. John Richter.)

Carl Sandburg with "luggage", arriving at 8 Henderson Pl. N.Y. 1955

Carl's shopping bag baggage contained all his needs for a longish stay; shirts, long johns, socks, hankies in one sack. The other held a dozen oranges, a quart of goat's milk, a fifth of Jack Daniels, and notebooks.

strings of the Spanish guitar and later the nylon strings, which closely emulate the gut in tone production, are more like the tissue of the human vocal chord in intonation, and therefore closer to the nuance, dynamics, and flexibility of the human voice itself.

Now Carl was a confirmed guitar man, and all his life he acquired guitars as he was able to afford them. His eye was caught by the physical beauty of the instrument, and his ear was caught by its gentle, dulcet voice. His heart was completely captured by the whole romance of the instrument. He called the guitar "a box of chosen woods." When he saw and heard a beautiful instrument, he wanted to hold it, run his eye lovingly along its lines, and run his fingers over its bouts, its fingerboard, its smooth, delicate neck. His poet's heart rejoiced over the beauty of shape, design, and workmanship. His ears admired the voice of the instrument, even if his old poet's hands could not coax enough music from it.

Carl's guitars came and went. He was not miserly about them; he did not hoard guitars so much as he boarded them. He was more custodian than owner of them. Actually, his own guitar needs were simple. For his sparse, almost primitive playing, a beat-up old timer which always lay on his piano was more than adequate. Thus, if he found someone worthy enough to give better voice to his finer instruments, he parted with them gladly.

One of Sandburg's earliest guitar gifts was to his own grandson, John Carl Steichen. The lad had been in the constant company of the Washburn twins at Connemara Farm from 1945 until 1952. It is inconceivable that an impressionable grandson of a poet would remain impervious to their allure, for they were made of fine woods and handsomely inlaid with gold leaf.

As soon as the delighted grandfather noticed that the little kid-fist could grasp the fingerboard of a guitar, one of the pear-shaped pair became his.

"Buppong gave it to me many years ago," John Carl wrote me in March 1968, "and I used it when I was studying with [Sophocles] Papas in Washington in 1961."

If "Buppong" sounds like baby talk, it is.

"John Carl tried to say 'Grandpa' when he was a baby, and it came out 'Buppong,'" explained Carl. "And among a few persons, that name clings."

The other Washburn went to two young friends in Washington,

Dr. Bill and Marjorie Braye. They were among the few who called Carl "Buppong." Marge often worked with Carl on manuscript chores, particularly the one-volume edition of *Abraham Lincoln,* published in 1954.

Marge died suddenly in 1966. Carl, himself only a year away from the end, was inconsolably grieved at the news. She had been like a daughter to him.

Carl was always on the prowl for guitar pals and duet partners, and for years, Marge was his Washington favorite. When he visited the capital, he knew where to find a good song session waiting for him.

It was several years after World War II that Sandburg began admiring the Spanish guitar. Once export trade began to open up, many excellent handcrafted instruments began arriving in the United States from the ateliers of Europe, particularly Spain and Germany. These works of the luthier's art were in constant demand and quickly snapped up by players aching all those war years for guitars worthy of the name "classic."

Though Marge loved the Washburn, she had been yearning wistfully for a Spanish guitar. To own one, a really fine one of distinguished name, workmanship, and beauty, could only be a dream. Such gems came high. But it was constantly on her mind.

And on her husband's. Dr. Bill was resolved to get his wife that guitar of her heart's desire. And he wanted it for her next birthday, barely a month off. But where to find one? He knew little of guitars.

He brought his problem to Carl, who not only volunteered to help him find such an instrument of proper dimensions, aspect, and lineage, but also to help pay for it; he knew their value. But more, he wanted a share of the pleasure of giving. When up New York way, he promised, he'd look around. When he began his search, he realized how fortuitously he had come by two apples of his eye only a few years back: the Augustine Mönch and the Martinez Esteso.

Carl pressed on with his inquiries, and he found to his frustration that while guitars were indeed becoming more available, there were more than enough eager purchasers waiting with poised checkbooks. Some of the guitars, too, were prohibitively expensive. Although Carl and Dr. Bill were splitting the cost, their budget was unbudgeable; and when a good buy appeared, someone else snapped it up immediately. The guitar grapevine was working overtime in those days.

Marge's birthday was drawing near. Carl's quest seemed doomed to failure. But at the eleventh hour, his search suddenly ended. He found *the* guitar. Moreover, he persuaded its owner to part with it—and it all happened virtually in his own backyard in New York.

It was in my house. It was my guitar. And again, it was a most fortuitous find: my guitar, too, was a Mönch!

I had always kept the precious instrument securely in its case, trusting it only to the better players among my friends who disdained to play on an instrument of less quality. When I was alone, I would slip it out and play it. It was like sneaking down to a secret place in the cellar for a special bottle of wine.

One day in early June 1958, Sandburg dropped in to see us at Henderson Place, catching me in the middle of private guitar practice on my Mönch. Carl came, saw, and pounced. Where had I been keeping that guitar all the while he'd known me? I pointed out that perhaps he had seen it and forgotten. Never mind. He was seeing it now, and he had to have it. There was much at stake: an approaching birthday, an anxious husband, a yearning wife, his solemn promise, and grief all around if he failed—or if I failed him. In a trice, the burden of responsibility had fallen from his shoulders to mine. "All right," I said, sighing deeply. "I will let you have it."

Like all guitars of noble lineage, my Mönch had its own story. The biography of this instrument began in Munich, Germany.

In 1950 my wife, Terry, was a top syndicated cartoonist for King Features as the creator of the first teen-age girl comic strip in the U.S., "Teena." She was chosen by the USO as one of a group of famous cartoonists to entertain with chalk-talks and audience participation acts for U.S. troop installations in Germany, particularly in and around Munich.

Munich! It may have been the encampment of thousands of U.S. troops, but to me, it was a spot in the world where two of the greatest masters of guitar-making lived and worked: Edgar Mönch and Hermann Hauser. How I envied my wife this great chance to meet the great luthiers. I was a cartoonist myself, but could not have joined the group. My deadlines were more complex, involving contracts with others than my syndicate. Next best was to enjoin my wife, on pain of finding a complete change of locks on our front door when she came home, not to dream of returning without a guitar from Munich out of the shops of Mönch or Hauser—or both, and hang the cost. We'd go in hock, if need be.

In Munich, Terry, at her first opportunity, made for the house of Hauser. She found it closed. A hausfrau next door approached her. "Nein, nein!" exclaimed the woman. "Gestorben!" Then, vigorously jabbing a finger upward, she added, "Himmel! Himmel!" (Heaven! Heaven!)

Having made a heaven on earth for so many in his lifetime on earth, Himmel above was where a luthier of Hauser's genius belonged. Terry had gone to him first; his was the bigger reputation, if the choice of the master Segovia counted for anything. For years, his best guitar was a Hauser. Paradoxically, the great Spanish guitarist had finally found his ideal Spanish guitar not in romantic Spain, but in Teutonic Germany.

From the disappointment at Hauser's to another disappointment at Mönch's: when Terry arrived there, she was glad to see that Mönch was not only alive, but busy, busy in his humming workshop. Guitars in profusion and in various stages of completion were everywhere: supine, on their sides, hanging—and strewn about, here, there—in every available space, half-tops, full-tops, full-backs, half-backs, necks, sides, shavings, varnish, gluepots.

"It was like a Picasso painting in his early Cubist period," Terry said of the seeming chaos. Too bad, Mönch said; he had not a single instrument available. All of them, in all their states, completed or not, were spoken for, not only by a guitar-awakening world outside, but by a regenerating Germany around him.

Of course, Mönch was glad to hear of his burgeoning reputation in the States, and especially in New York among the cognoscenti of the classic guitar society. But much flattery got Terry nowhere. Mönch spoke good English; especially could he enunciate the word "sorry," clearly and forcibly. Then Terry turned on the waterworks, telling him in tones of high *schmerz* a lugubrious tale of a husband languishing in New York, pining piteously for a creation from this master luthier. It won him over, just as a similar story over the same Mönch won me over, eight years later.

Mönch took a beautiful example of his work from off a rack and held it up, turning it this way and that. "I have just completed this guitar for somebody here in Munich," he said. "He has been waiting six months for it, but he is a good friend and can wait a little longer. All right, I will let you have it."

"All right, I will let you have it," I said to Carl Sandburg eight years later.

Thus, Marge's and Dr. Bill's Buppong had come through, and there was happiness all around. As for me, I moped around the house, bereft, bothered, and bewildered without my beautiful Mönch. Nobody but Sandburg could have pried it away from me.

Wrote Carl soon after: "Greg Old Hoss—that guitar you let go so graciously pleases to perfection. For this one deed, St. Peter may let us in.—Old Hoss Carlos."

Antonita Martinez, a former flamenco dancer, and her husband and partner, Juan, a crack flamenco guitarist, opened a walk-up restaurant on West Fifty-second Street in one of the years between the end of the Spanish Civil War and the beginning of World War II. Not surprisingly, they called the place El Flamenco. Antonita's *paella a la Valenciana* was excellent. Juan's flamenco guitar noodling was authentic. Entertainment at El Flamenco was spontaneous. Carmen Amaya herself exploded into dance there many times between helpings of paella; the great Sabicas streamed out many a *rasgueado* roll on his flamenco guitar.

One banner evening I took Carl Sandburg to dinner at El Flamenco. Juan and Antonita Martinez, simple, folkloric, were Sandburg's kind of people; and the white haired, amiable old gentleman—*el gran poeta Americano* San-bur-r-r—became their respected Don Carlos.

I had ordered a paella for two, and we could hear the garlic kernels sizzling merrily in the age-blackened pan of hot olive oil, presided over by Señora Martinez. As she made her magic in the kitchen, Juan created his own magic on the guitar, seated in a booth off to a corner of the dining area. To regulars of El Flamenco, this spot was known as *la mesa de la familia,* where not only family, but close friends were also privileged to sit. There Carl and I were invited to sit after we had dispatched the paella at our own table. I had earned the honor only after five years of steady attendance at El Flamenco; Carl Sandburg made it the first night.

The booth seated three on each side, and two, with chairs drawn up to it, at the open end. Gradually, the restaurant was becoming a microcosm of flamenco Spain: the gypsies were arriving at a time when other restaurants in New York were putting their chairs on the tables. A lean, dark-haired girl appeared at the door, flashed a look around the room, and glided over to our table. She was hawk-faced, arch-necked, spit-curled; if she wasn't a flamenco dancer, then I would have to look again at a Goya and deny that I see Spain in his every brushstroke. She was a dancer; Goya's brushstrokes would not lie. Close behind the dancer arrived two young men. One was a male counterpart of the girl, and he slipped hiplessly into a place at the table next to her. Now there were three at Martinez's side of the table. Although that would normally be the limit of space, one more hipless wonder could fit in with ease, and one did a few minutes later. He was even smaller than the two dancers, a little older and not as strikingly handsome. He was carrying a multi-labeled guitar case, which bespoke of travels around the world as guitarist for a Spanish dance company. Gently, he set the case down and reverently extracted a guitar. There was a gasp of admiration, mine overpowering the others. Sandburg, at his first flamenco experience, saw only a plain, unadorned box of featherweight construction all in blond woods, and thus saw nothing to marvel at. That was before he heard it.

The guitarist crashed his hand down across the strings in a spine-tingling *rasgueado.* The boy and girl rose, and together wove their bodies in and out of several *compasas sevillanas;* from out of nowhere, castanets appeared in their hands. Then the castanets disappeared, and the hands were used in sharp *palmadas* and *pitos.* The dancers raised their untrained, barely adult voices in wails of *cante* flamenco.

What did Sandburg know of flamenco? Nothing. What did he feel of flamenco? Everything. His response was instant, intuitive; it was another culture, another tradition, another ethos, perhaps, but one with the people and of a common core.

We were soon joined by Mr. and Mrs. Oliver La Farge, El Flamenco regulars when they were in New York on a visit from their home in Santa Fe, New Mexico. Author of such novels as *Sparks Fly Upward* and *Laughing Boy,* La Farge, always a guitar enthusiast, was organizer and president of the Santa Fe Guitar Society. He sought out the guitar wherever he stopped. El Flamenco was the place in New York.

The two scriveners were delighted and amazed to meet each other in so unlikely a setting as a flamenco joint. La Farge spoke fluent

Spanish, which embraced also the careless, carefree Andalusian idiom of our flamenco friends at the table. My high school Castilian was useless among them; only Martinez could say a few basic, elementary English words. So La Farge's presence was most useful.

The guitarist swept all five fingers of his right hand across the strings in a final chord. Then, holding it by the top of the neck, he lifted the guitar on high for all to see. Unlike the dark flashing eyes and black sheen of spit-curled hair connoting the Spanish complexion, the flamenco guitar is blond. Aside from the fingerboard, tuning pegs, and bridge, which are black, the typical flamenco guitar is blond all over, in contrast to the Spanish classic guitar, whose only light-colored wood is the soundboard. These pale spruce woods are not only light in color, but also in weight, imparting to the flamenco guitar its characteristic sharp, brilliant, percussive timbre. The guitar came from the shop of Domingo Esteso of Madrid—the "old man," as the guitarists referred to him, to distinguish his works from those turned out by his nephews (Los Sobrinos Esteso) after the "old man" died in the mid-forties.

"Ask the young man if he wants to sell the guitar," Carl said to La Farge.

Like all aficionados, especially the newly afflicted, Sandburg was going over his head, and he knew it. What could an old former banjo player and now the user of a heavy steel-stringed American-make guitar want with a featherweight blond flamenco guitar? He was aware that with his own fingers, he could not coax from it the fire he had just heard. But he knew it lay in the box, and that was enough for him. The fever was on him, and he had to have that guitar, his very first Spanish guitar.

La Farge relayed the offer to the guitarist. There was an exchange between them replete with the Andalusian barking sound and the perverse pronouncing of letters and words in direct opposition to the dictums of the pure Castilian. The guitarist was willing to sell, though he hated to part with so fine an instrument. But he had others in his hotel room. Yes, he would be proud to know that *el gran poeta Americano* Sanbur-r-r was the possessor of a guitar he once possessed. Did the gentleman know the value of a guitar such as this one of so fine a lineage?

Sandburg looked at me and winked. "cinco centavos [five cents]," he said huskily. The inside joke eluded and alarmed the Spaniards.

Not La Farge, though. He wasn't in on the joke, but he saw the wink. Sandburg chuckled off his bid, and the talk turned seriously to *dinero*.

"He says he paid 18,500 *pesetas* in Madrid, and he will let you have it for that price. You would be getting it duty-free," relayed La Farge. "But hold on; I'm sure we can strike a better bargain." Then he turned to the guitarist, and the barking resumed. Carl was shaking his head; he did not know the rate of exchange between the U.S. dollar and the Spanish *peseta* any more than he did the *satang* of Thailand. The barking trailed off; there was a nodding of heads and smiles between La Farge and the guitarist.

"Well," the writer said, "I got him down to sixteen-five. That's a good buy for such a great instrument, and I think you ought to grab it."

The people of Spain, the language of Spain, the music of Spain, the food of Spain—all of these Sandburg encountered at El Flamenco in one night. Now he would have a brush with its monetary system. He reached into his pocket, pulled out a sheaf of bills, and slowly began counting out twenty-, ten-, and five-dollar bills, up to $275.

The deal was consummated, and Sandburg now had his first Spanish guitar, without case, however. The young guitarist might rationalize parting with one of his beloved instruments, but he would never give up his battered old case, whose scores of labels from all parts of the world depicted the whole history of his career.

Sandburg could not contain his joy on his first visit to El Flamenco; he got to sit at the boss's table and then to acquire an authentic Esteso—one of the few remaining by the "old man" of Madrid. He thanked La Farge effusively for his help. He had a real bargain, he was assured by all.

Martinez went into his kitchen and came out with a large piece of brown wrapping paper and some string, and he swathed the guitar with it, making it into the image of a voluptuously shaped mummy.

We left with the smell of Spain in our clothes and its sounds still in our ears. Wrapped in the brown paper rested more of the sound, waiting to be brought to life. Sandburg, like his Rootabaga hero Henry Hagglyhoagly, now possessed a real Spanish guitar. "It ain't a mandolin," Henry Hagglyhoagly proudly said. "It ain't a mouth organ, nor an accordion, nor a concertina nor a fiddle. It is a guitar, a Spanish Spinnish Splishy guitar made special."

For almost seven years, the Esteso remained in a case at Connemara, like a museum piece to look at, but not to touch. In the meantime, Carl acquired another Spanish guitar, this one a classic model made by Monch. With this magnificent guitar, I'm sure Sandburg had many moments, if not hours. At least, I've seen photos of him in which I could spot the Mönch as easily as I could Sandburg's phizzog. Ironically, while the Esteso's tuning head suggested a no-nonsense, ungadgety simplicity as compared to the gear-wheel system of the modern machine-head, it is always a baffling business trying to tune such an instrument, unless you are around flamenco guitars a lot. Thus, it is entirely possible that Sandburg did not touch the Esteso, simply because he couldn't tune it. Anyway, there were always other guitars around, like that beat-up old wire-stringed box which he kept on the top of the piano.

The Esteso lay silent like a Sleeping Beauty. Clearly, Sandburg was not her Prince Charming, and he sensed the loss, the waste. "That's too good an instrument to just lie there," he said to me one day in the summer of 1957 via long distance from Flat Rock. "Some good player oughta have it." And it was then that he resolved to end the Big Sleep of the Esteso. He decided to donate his flamenco guitar to our Society of the Classic Guitar. True to his word, when next he came to New York, he delivered the instrument to me at Henderson Place, stayed a while, and then fled to keep many appointments.

Carl left me to ponder what to do with the bonanza. What would be his wishes as to its disposition? I wrote him at Flat Rock, and he answered me promptly: "The Esteso guitar I left with you is for any purpose whatsoever that you and the officers of The Society of the Classic Guitar may designate. You can sell it, you can offer it as a prize and make an award of it. I have so complete a confidence in you and Bobri that I trust you two as Lincoln did Grant and Sherman after he found them."

We did all three things Sandburg suggested. First, we sold the guitar for substantially more than Sandburg had paid for it at El Flamenco seven years before; it was in fine condition and had become even more valuable as an instrument of ever-increasing rarity. Then we split the money into two prizes to be awarded the composer of the best set of variations on the theme of an American folk song, to be published in an All-American issue of *The Guitar Review*. For the theme around which the contestants would weave their variations, we dipped into Sandburg's *American Songbag* and came up with "Colorado Trail," as American a song as exists, with a melody line at once beautiful and viable for the task at hand. The contest was international; our office was deluged with hundreds of manuscripts from the world over, including such non-Western, noncowboy countries as Japan, Israel, Egypt, and others way, way off the Colorado Trail.

In the winter of 1959, we announced the results of our competition. It was cosmopolitan from start to finish. Judging of the contest was headed by Andrés Segovia of Spain and Vladimir Bobri, Russian émigré; first prize winner was John W. Duarte of London, England; runner-up was James Yoghourtian of Racine, Wisconsin, son of Armenian immigrants; the prize money was provided through the sale of a flamenco guitar made in Madrid and donated to The Society of the Classic Guitar by the son of a Swedish immigrant; the purchaser of the guitar was John C. Tanno of Phoenix, Arizona, guitar pedagogue and historian, and first-generation Italian; and Sandburg's wishes were first put into motion by another first generation ditto.

Thus ended the saga of the Sandburg Spanish, Spinnish, Splishy Esteso guitar, truly a box of chosen wood.

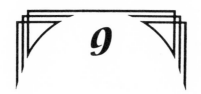

The Portable Companion

THE GUITAR IS AN INSTRUMENT pleasant to hear and to be near, delightful to hold and behold, but a nuisance to carry.

Carl Sandburg once described it as "weighing less than a newborn infant." Correct. But let us be careful to make clear that when the precious instrument is snugged away safely in its case in plush padding, our "newborn infant" now weighs as much as a small boy.

Sandburg's poem further pays grateful tribute to the guitar's weightlessness when he dubs it "a portable companion." It is portable, yes, but only in the sense that a piano is not.

Carl needed a portable instrument in the days when he was crisscrossing the United States, giving recitals and readings. It was his living, this work, a mainstay of his family's existence. His writing was not yet paying off, and he would perform for anybody who would pay his fee of a hundred dollars a performance. Very early in his troubadour days, it was the banjo that accompanied him on trains and in song; later it was the guitar. He found willing hands to carry the guitar on concert trails as his fame grew. Even though he had many helpful porters waiting for him at his stops, there was still the ordeal of getting the awkwardly shaped burden out of plane, bus, or train, needling it through the narrow aisles, while the other hand managed a piece of luggage, a suitcase, perhaps. Most aisles are too narrow to accommodate both guitar and luggage, so one of them must be shifted to the front, and it is usually the guitar. The distance between the front end of the guitar neck and the rear end of a person ahead is difficult to judge. In point of fact, the prow of the pesky guitar, which protrudes like the proboscis of a platypus, is usually prodding the preceding passenger in the posterior.

Carl's dependence on a guitar had little to do with its robustness of timbres and carrying power. Any fairly good playable instrument would do for him. When guitar players, guitar societies, and guitar centers began to flourish in the late forties, Sandburg began to leave his guitar at home. The map of the U.S. was soon dotted with admirers ready to drop everything when their great friend Carl Sandburg was passing through. In a matter of minutes, a guitar would be in his hands if he needed one.

And he always did. Scarcely a function in his honor was ever complete without the old troubadour booming out a few songs. But he seldom arrived with a guitar, even when he knew that something in the way of music was expected of him. And he was always happy to oblige, but inevitably, there came the usual scurrying about town to borrow a guitar.

Carl's love for the guitar had not in the least diminished. He had not given up his portable companion. He'd simply given up porting it.

Newspapers always carried stories of Sandburg's presence at a dinner or some other function, quoting some of his speech, and then winding up with: "Someone in the audience called out 'Give us a song, Carl,' and somebody brought out a guitar."

Somebody. Somebody who?

Well, if it happened in New York between 1949 and 1962, that anonymous, unsung Somebody would be me.

In those thirteen years, I was poised at any hour for The Sudden Sandburg Summons; neither rain, nor sleet, nor dark of night could stay me in my delivery of a guitar to him on his appointed rounds. I was now the companionable porter of his portable companion.

In November 1950, The Museum of Modern Art in New York conducted a series on American poetry. Prominent poets were invited to give readings of their works in the red plush upholstered auditorium in the basement of the museum. One poet with a special cachet was especially invited to participate in the series: at the close of his readings, the announcement read, he would sing some American folk songs with guitar. How else would Carl Sandburg be allowed to leave the stage at the close of his readings?

The songs Sandburg sang that night were one hundred percent American; but the guitar he used was first-generation American, of Spanish lineage, classic model, made in the USA, in the little town of Bethlehem, Pennsylvania, by the old house of C. F. Martin. The guitar was a beauty, bright and shiny, and best of all, sturdily made, so that there was little danger of cracking due to atmospheric changes or damage from rough treatment. It was a good knockabout, "second" guitar; but after one got the feel of its fingerboard and control of its dynamics, it came close to becoming one's number one guitar. How do I know these intimacies? Because it was my guitar, one of the several which Carl Sandburg borrowed from me whenever he needed one in New York.

Sandburg, the guitar, and I taxied to the museum, where Carl went to await his cue backstage. I awaited his appearance from my seat in the audience. This was my first time to see Sandburg in public performance on such a large scale and under such distinguished auspices. That went for my guitar, too.

Guitar and Sandburg looked and sounded great. Both shone brightly; even Carl's blue serge suit gave off interesting light effects.

In November 1950, Sandburg was approaching his seventy-third year. At that age, few men have maintained memory boxes that have not begun to come apart at the joints. Carl's memory, however, was intact, and his capacity for coming up with words of songs, amazing. But it was no great feat for him. The earthly practice of committing words to memory was not for him. He had an *arrangement*. When words would not come to him, he simply looked up and waited.

Carl had cut through several songs like butter. Now he was on "The Cowboy's Lament," and had droned out the line "O beat the drum slowly . . ." There, he had inserted a *rallentando;* but after an inordinate delay, it had become an actual stop. He looked up and waited. Soon, the words to the next line would appear on that *great big teleprompter* in the sky. But they were late in coming if they were coming at all. He strained his neck forward and upward, squinted and frowned. The giant screen was blank, due, no doubt, to a "delay caused by operational difficulties" in *the studio.*

Though his singing had stopped, his guitar plucking continued, vamping till ready for the next line. Then giving up all hope of help from Up There, Carl turned to the audience and looked searchingly into it. Still plucking away at the chord where the breakdown had occurred, he gave out a few "haws," and called out: "Hey, d'Alez-z-zio! Holler out the next line, will you?"

Anonymous—nay, a nonentity—I had entered the citadel of the pacemakers and the tastemakers of modern art, and now, with my name ringing throughout the galleries, echoing and reechoing among the Gauguins, Picassos, Modiglianis, Chagalls, I had suddenly become the man of the hour who would save the day.

Heads began to swivel, shoulders shifted. Who was d'Alez-z-zio? *Where* was d'Alez-z-zio? Carl called out again: "Can you give me the next line, Gregory?" I sat frozen with fear, wretched in defeat. For the life of me, I could not throw out the lifeline. The tragic streets of Laredo were *terra incognita* to me.

Before I could rise to my feet and apologetically deliver my "Gregorian Can't," a voice broke into the buzzing from somewhere in the audience. It was loud and clear, male, mature:

> *Play the dead march as they carry me along,*
> *Put branches of roses all over my . . .*

Carl interrupted: "I got it now," he said. "Thanks, Greg." Past the bottleneck now, he got through the song and the remainder of the concert with no further mishap.

Somewhere in the departing crowd, the other d'Alessio was probably receiving the admiring glances of those who had been seated in his near vicinity and knew him to be the real hero of the evening, if not the real d'Alessio. Anyway, I was grateful to him, whoever he was, just as Carl was grateful to me, as he told me later. I never set him straight on it. Let it be, let it be, I thought. But I did resolve to brush up on "The Cowboy's Lament" and other songs Carl often sang, just in case.

Painting being my trade, I am often asked, "Are any of your works in The Museum of Modern Art?" I always answer: "No, but my name was hollered out loud in it once."

"Spot the Guitar!" That was the name of the game played by the friends of Carl Sandburg whenever he appeared in any visual media in his most familiar pose: holding a guitar.

In the 1950s, guitar pals in Washington, New York, Chicago, and other cities might open up their newspapers or magazines, or turn on their television sets and find Carl, guitar across his lap.

"That's my Ramirez!" its proud owner would exclaim. "That's my Mönch!" another would call. "That's my Esteso!" still another beamed.

"That's my Martin!" That's what I exclaimed when I caught Carl Sandburg on Arthur Godfrey's show one evening.

He used my guitar that night. I'd delivered it in person. Had I wished, I could have stuck around and seen the show live from the wings, but I preferred to hurry home and watch it with the Missus and friends, to see how Carl came over on our own set.

From the looks of Carl on screen, it seemed that he'd spurned makeup. His face caught every light in the studio. These were the days before color television but Sandburg's ruddiness came through anyway. None of it was lost in translation into black and white.

If a fastidious cameraman was disturbed by the light gone wild on Sandburg's phizzog, he must have blown his top when he saw the havoc wrought by the lights on my shiny, flashy Martin. Here was where a real makeup job was needed—beginning with several coats of dulling spray. With every shift of the guitar, the mirrorlike surfaces sent out flashes of light that seared the screen, the viewers' eyes, and the cameraman's soul. Indeed, my Martin easily outshone everybody that night—even Sandburg's famous phizzog.

As if this quasi-catastrophe were not enough, everyone was aware of it but Carl, who was seated behind the trouble and unconsciously controlling it. Indeed, a more serious hazard was developing. It seemed that a rigid rule of split-second timing was beginning to split at the seams. The number one of television's sacred cows was about to be led to the abattoir: a commercial would have to go by the board, while Sandburg kept his position center screen, singing, reminiscing, storytelling, as if there were no tomorrow or a CBS business office.

Down went the commercial, and now Carl was on his way to whittle down, if not entirely preempt, the time of the next one. Only the president of the United States announcing a clear and present danger; God; and in this case, Godfrey, could stay the inexorable commercial. But Godfrey seemed almost as unperturbed over the clear and present danger of a sacrificed commercial as Carl was blithely unaware of it. There was no question of Godfrey's awe and fascination with the white-haired troubadour droning away before him, plucking at the guitar. He allowed Carl to go on.

Now, to all intents and purposes, Carl seemed to have come to the end of a many-versed song and his part in the show; Godfrey moved to make appropriate wind-up remarks. But Carl was already on his next song.

"From out of the Wes-s-t of the 1880s," he boomed, "comes along the song 'Hal-lelujah I'm a Bum . . .' " Up came his guitar; down went the next commercial. The last hallelujah at last faded away, and Godfrey got on mike before Carl could get another song under way. But if Arthur felt any panic or doom, he gave no indication of it. If the television industry was crumbling, it was happening on his own show, at least. Always a nonconformist in those earlier days of TV, Godfrey may even have been secretly enjoying it all; but above all, he was always the gracious, breezy Godfrey.

Carl now turned his attention to Godfrey. This could be the moment when the flood of dammed-up commercials might be loosed upon the air. But it was not in Godfrey to so banish Carl from the screen. Unruffled, he said: "I think we have time for one more, Carl; but a short one—a *very* short one."

That's the story of the debut of my Martin guitar on television, with Carl Sandburg singing a few songs. It was nothing earthshaking to Carl, nothing he didn't do every day, anyway, in a quiet room, anywhere he happened to be, where time stood still for him, where no commercials were lined up awaiting their turn.

One day, my friend Bobri, president of The Society of the Classic Guitar, espied my Martin standing on a rack off to a corner of the room in which we were sitting. I had retired my Martin as a loan-out instrument, particularly for TV appearances: too shiny. Mr. B, as I always called him, picked up the guitar gingerly by the top of its neck, held it off from him disdainfully, and inspected it, turning it this way and that for the effect of light on its body.

"This guitar-r-r," he said loftily, in accents of an émigré aristocrat from White Holy Russia—"this guitar-r-r is dor-r-rty."

Dirty, no; not in the sense that it was unclean. It was simply uncleaned. I had not passed a cloth over it for months, not after

Sandburg had started using the once-shiny instrument. I just could not bring myself to wipe off his fingerprints.

Or Segovia's. The Maestro had had and would continue to have contact with the Martin. It was hardly the quality of guitar that he would entrust to the demands of a concert performance, but as an instrument he could reach over and pick up, play, puff his pipe over, speak and laugh past, rest his arms upon, he could ask for nothing better during an evening visit at my house. Other top-notch guitarists had played it. Would I therefore be likely to remove so patrician a patina from my modest Martin? For as long a time as the guitar might remain intact, I resolved, it would never feel the pressure of chamois cloth to disturb the precious prints. By now, they must be buried beneath layers of other prints, but that did not make them less ever-present. They were like the underpainting of a Rembrandt, invisible, but giving meaning to the visible.

The Missus and I took a trip to Florida that year. Since I am never without a guitar whenever I leave home for any protracted period, I toted along the dor-r-rty Martin, its distinguished fingerprints still undisturbed, of course. We stayed a month, and despite the capriciousness of a Florida winter, the guitar structurally and cosmetically remained complete and entire. At Grand Central, on our return, our porter lined up our luggage along the platform. The porter completed his job and reentered the car just before we detrained. At that moment when the luggage was unguarded, unwatched—it fell prey to a sneak thief. At least he was romantic; he stole only the guitar.

But in taking my prized guitar, he took away something more precious—the invisible finger traces of memory.

We stood at the open door one raw winter day as the January chill quickly began to fill the small foyer. Sandburg, bundled up, muffler past his ears up to his white hair, was about to leave. He was due at a private dinner-preview of *The Family of Man,* the exhibition of photographs selected by his brother-in-law Edward Steichen at The Museum of Modern Art.

Snow threatened. It was a sure thing for later in the evening. I surveyed Carl from dark, snap-brimmed hat to rubbered feet. He had everything but a guitar.

That's what I said. "You have everything but a guitar." It was a reminder. "I would be glad to carry one along for you to the dinner." And leave directly, I almost added; this was one function where Carl was not free to take along a pal.

I almost added: "I'd rather get the job over with now than later, when I will most probably be summoned out of my warm bed and into the blizzard of the night." I was certain that if this evening ran true to form, not only would there be a clamor for a "few songs" from Carl, but Carl himself would wish a guitar were around. It was inevitable that the desire to hear *himself* sing would be strong upon him.

"No, no," he assured me. "This is one time I'm sure there'll be no need for a guitar. All I'm expected to do is read my *Family of Man* prologue in the book; and I guess the dinner will break up just after."

Not believing one word of it, I accompanied Carl out into the street to the corner of East End Avenue and Eighty-sixth Street. I flagged him a taxi, saw him into it, and scurried back to the house, already frozen to the bone, as the first snowflake of the promised storm landed on my nose with a gentle thud. I went directly to my guitar, the Augustine, checked it, inspected it carefully, sounded the strings, wrapped the chamois cloth lovingly around the soundhole, and restored the instrument snugly to its case. Then I settled into a chair before the television set. I would hold off on bed for a while. I waited, waited . . .

At the moment when the weatherman was announcing that the storm was on its way, the summons came.

"Mr. d'Ale-z-z-z-io?" intoned a voice over the phone, clearly not Sandburg's—but imitating Sandburg's juicy pronunciation of my name. The dinner and ceremonies and speeches were over, he continued, "and all of us here thought it would be nice if Mr. Sandburg could sing a few songs."

"And you wonder if I could get a guitar over there right away," I filled in.

"Why, yes!" he said in surprise.

"Directly," I answered cheerfully, as the weatherman on television predicted ten inches of snow by morning. I stepped out into the snowy night with Carl's guitar.

In December 1957, the three of us arrived at another great party, just a little late. I was in the center, with Carl Sandburg at my left arm; on my right arm was the Augustine guitar. Together, we entered Toots Shor's. From the size of the mob milling about, it would seem that most of the guests had already arrived.

The television industry had just voted "See It Now" the top documentary show of the year. Celebrating the honor, Edward R. Murrow, moderator, reporter, interviewer, and commentator, and Fred W. Friendly, CBS producer, promptly arranged a party in Toots Shor's upstairs dining room.

One of the great episodes of "See It Now" featured Carl Sandburg. Murrow and his crew had gone down to Flat Rock to film Carl. Murrow was as skilled and intelligent an interviewer of poets as he was of actors and physicists. He had done episodes of "See It Now" with Danny Kaye and J. Robert Oppenheimer, and both were present at the party.

I had been heartily and enthusiastically invited to the party by Carl, and I wouldn't have cared if it *was* because of my services as a guitar toter-lender, either. But it wasn't. Carl, ever gracious, introduced me around as he would any guitar pal.

The room was teeming with celebrities, characters I'd always looked up to, images on screen or in print or names in the news. Now, as Carl and I walked among them, I found myself looking up *at* them. Sandburg, a good 5′ 11″ himself, and I, a respectable 5′ 8½″ in my subtly built-up heels, would be dismissed by these giant redwoods as mere saplings. There was Fred W. Friendly himself, not only tall, but of great girth. If his position as a CBS production chief could fail to establish him as a commanding figure, his size would. Danny Kaye was slender, tall, graceful, bubbly, always on. Eric Sevareid was cool, distant. Robert Oppenheimer was reed-thin, still young, hair shot with gray, blue eyes with a great hurt in them. Edward R. Murrow was blue-jowled, with a ravaged face, already a cadaver, and smoking, smoking, smoking.

If the party did not start with Sandburg, it ended with him. Now I was snapping open the hasps of the case and handing him the Augustine. He stood on a raised platform, and started to strum the guitar. Conversations stopped in mid-sentence. The buzz and hum of a hundred voices slowly died away to just one, Sandburg's. Then, the silence gathered in, and he began to sing.

*   *   *   *

Thus ran a newspaper account the day after Carl Sandburg received the Yeshiva University Humanities Award in April 1956: "Then, at the close of the ceremonies, someone handed a guitar to Sandburg and he sang a few songs. . . ." The someone: me; the guitar: mine.

For this one, Terry and I received an engraved invitation from William Jovanovich, president of Carl's publishers Harcourt Brace and (now) Jovanovich. We sat at the company table with Carl's other friends and colleagues. It was a mammoth affair, impossible to hold anywhere else but at the Waldorf Astoria Hotel. The Grand Ballroom was a shimmering sea of handsomely gowned women, liberally speckled with men in black tuxedos.

In the dark suit and dark bow tie that passed for his tuxedo outfit, Carl rose to sing from his central and honored position at the speakers' table. Idly, he essayed a few chords within the first three frets of the fingerboard of the guitar: C major, G7, D major; then abruptly he left the first position and went down to the fifth fret for his All-Purpose Chord. I called it that because it seemed to fit any harmonic line, even if I could not identify it yet in my chord book.

With this background, he began to speak: "I want you to know, ladies and gentlemen, that I am a full-fledged member—an honorary member, if you please—of The New York Classic Guitar Society." He stepped up his playing dramatically. "And not only am I in the company tonight of the esteemed secretary of the society, Gregory d'Ale-z-z-z-i-ohhh, I am also privileged to be using his fine Augustine guitar." He raised the instrument on high for a moment, brought it down again, and resumed his chording. Then he launched into his songs.

Whatever Carl sang that night, I cannot remember, for the simple reason that I couldn't hear what he sang. My head was spinning, my ears were ringing. All I could hear was the sweet echo-h-h of d'Ale-z-z-z-i-ohhh as it bounced back and forth from crystal chandelier to crystal chandelier, reverberating from rafter to rafter in the elegance of the Waldorf Grand ballroom. To the last "ohhh" I savored the echo; and then I heard the audience applaud Sandburg's last song, and the evening was over.

In the Grand Ballroom, that is. When Sandburg joined us at our table, he invited all to join him for a drink and perhaps a few more songs in his elegant suite high up in the Waldorf Tower, provided for him by the university. Along the way, we picked up more friends of Sandburg's. We grew into a group of goodly size on our way up to the Tower.

A bottle of Jack Daniels appeared first, closely followed by the guitar. Now Carl was no longer the soloist he had been downstairs in the Grand Ballroom. Any number could join—and did. When an old familiar song was begun, all present went lustily into action, innocently displeasing the Tower regulars who were trying to get in their required hours of expensive sleep.

Came the knock, restrained, but indignant. It was the hall clerk, and he swept the room with an opprobrious and searching eye; then ah-ha!—he fixed it with triumph on the mischievous-looking old man with the guitar in his lap who, only a short hour or so ago, had been heaped with honors, kudos, and cheers by a great university.

Now, in his lofty tower, Carl was being dressed down by a lowly hall clerk—*sic transit gloria mundi*—and so soon! Like a saint in an old Byzantine icon, Carl raised his hand in a three-fingered gesture of peace. The noise would cease and desist, he promised; and soon after, the guests departed.

Ah—what a pity; a party going so well, then so abruptly aborted; songs that never got sung; Jack Daniels that never got drunk. It saddened Carl; but in the name of humanity, it had to be done. After all, what else could the winner of a humanities award do?

It is about two A.M., and Sandburg and I have departed the encroaching confines of a smoky, noisy party in a studio apartment in Manhattan's east mid-sixties. We're standing on the sidewalk, breathing in the clear, crisp, untroubled, unpolluted New York air of the mid-fifties. It has been a long night, and I am tired. I have been sitting for hours, but my legs are rubbery under me; I have been carrying the guitar for only a few minutes, but my arm is rubbery, too, already stretched to aching capacity by the guitar in its heavy case.

I spy a taxi in the distance, headed our way, and I wave my free arm. The taxi answers affirmatively with its yellow blinker light and speeds up. I hope Carl, too, is bushed enough to forget for once his mania for walking, especially late at night along empty streets, and enter the taxi with me for a quick trip home. But as my yellow-and-checkered rescuing angel slows down at the curb, Carl waves it on, and a curse that only a New York hackie can utter breaks the quiet of the New York night, echoing among its buildings.

Carl slips his hand under the handle of the guitar case. Now he has dislodged my hand, and the guitar has shifted from my tenuous grasp into his firm one.

"I'll carry it," he says quietly.

We begin our walk, Carl now with the portable companion. I mumble a protest, too faint to carry conviction.

Carl says, "I don't mind; you've had a hard night. But this fresh air will do you good!" And he quickens his step.

The Telephone Hour

CARL SANDBURG'S ARRIVAL at Henderson Place knocked out all other news that might have been humming along the New York literary and folk-song grapevine for the following few days. It seemed that as soon as he dropped his two shopping bags inside our vestibule, the whole world knew where he could be found.

And phoned and phoned and phoned. All kinds of calls began to pour in from friends, fellow folk singers and litterateurs, business associates, "family," very old and solidly entrenched friends, and a few crackpots. It was I who attempted diligently to take them all, for there was no telephone in Carl's room.

I felt obliged to exercise a prudent amount of editing of his phone messages. Were he to take each and every call, he would spend the day trudging down to the phone in my studio one floor below, then making the laborious ascent back to his room. Surely, I reckoned, he would now be forced to resort to his "resting" method of climbing stairs, and most likely—the calls being so numerous—he would often be caught in mid-flight by another call.

Despite my discreet screening of Carl's calls, there were enough of them to keep him descending and mounting the eighteen steps a good part of his working time. It was our assumption that he was bearing up under his ups and downs in deference to our hospitality, as any polite guest would. Despite his assurance that there was "nothin' wrong with the old ticker," I arranged with the phone company to install an extension in his room without delay.

Now Carl had his own phone—an extension, to be sure—but at least it precluded the constant climbing and all that loss of time. But it had not occurred to me, in my zealous haste to better accommodate my guest, that the telephone bell that tolled for me would also toll for him. The tolls for me began relentlessly and punctually when the business day began—at nine A.M. This is a price I still pay, though I am no businessman, for the joy of my multifarious activities.

When Carl presented himself at breakfast the morning following the installation of his phone, I noted instantly that there must be something amiss. He was not his beaming and cheery self. I'd suspected that there might be something wrong even before I'd seen him because of something I had not heard: the sound as of a sudden stumbling on the last few steps just outside our kitchen—mock-tripping that never failed to give us a start of apprehension. It was a rascally prank Carl loved to play on us. And we always fell for it, thinking: *this* time it's the real thing! But any annoyance we might have felt was dispelled when we saw him tall, straight, and whole, and chuckling mischievously, not violently sprawled at the bottom of the stairs.

Clearly, Carl was not in any kind of a jovial mood that morning, and I knew why: The telephone had taken its toll on him in the form of lost sleep—precious sleep that came to him only in the morning hours, the kind of sleep that one can ill afford to lose. Carl was a notorious night owl, counting on that morning sleep, if only for a few solid hours. It was enough to set him up for the day and get him through all hours of the night.

"Now about that phone you put in upstairs," Carl said, punctuating each word with a dunk of a crust of liberally buttered Italian bread into a large mug of expresso coffee. "I appreciate your thoughtfulness, but I want to repeat that those stairs don't bother me at all. So you can just get the phone out of there and holler up when the calls are for me." Once again, Carl brushed aside our solicitude over matters of his health. Like Picasso at eighty, Sandburg had decided to remain thirty for the rest of his life.

Unlike Picasso, Sandburg was accessible. Soon after Carl had spurned our efforts to preserve his physical energy, we received another firm but gentle instruction—this time, to summon him down for any and all phone calls. I had apologized to him one morning for having allowed a call which I'd deemed of doubtful importance to get through to him; the caller sounded like a crackpot, or at best, a pest, and probably not worth Carl's trip up and down those stairs. He rolled his eyes up and around.

"Oh," he said, waving his stump of a cheroot around in a gesture of generosity. "Let 'em come—let 'em come. I want to take them all." And there rested the last remnant of our worrying and fussing about Sandburg's ticker, digestion, comfort, privacy—or anything else.

My release from the self-imposed responsibility of having to screen Carl's phone calls was not only a relief, but a blessing in disguise, and it was beginning to pay off. My telephone rested at arm's length on the upper right corner of my tilting king-sized drawing table, set against a ledge to prevent it from sliding down into my drawing arm and thus ruining any deathless line that might have been in the making. Each time Carl arrived for a phone call, there we were—artist and subject—vis-à-vis. I couldn't miss.

It was an artist's dream. How often does a man who is a national monument walk into an artist's sights, perfectly framed? Pushing aside the cartoon I was working on, I'd grab any piece of paper handy (once, I drew Carl on the other side of a cartoon) and go to work on his remarkable features. Often, Carl would be wearing his battered city-desk green visor. As he sat there at the phone, pencil working, cheroot in mouth, he looked like a crusty old rewrite man taking a story from a legman calling from Chicago's South Side.

I always tried to keep my sketching of Carl as unobtrusive as possible. Thus, I never showed him the results of his unscheduled sittings there before me at the corner of my drawing table; but if I thought he was unaware that his famous phizzog was under my scrutiny and probing pencil, I was soon disabused of that idea. One day, having completed a phone call and restored receiver to cradle, he looked up at me through his green visor, and said, "Let me see that one."

Reluctantly, and with some trepidation, I handed over the sketch. He sighed a deep "Hmmm," then pushed the visor up from his forehead and away from his eyes. He held up the small oblong of

Bristol board before him, the better to inspect the drawing without the green glaze of the visor over it. He said wryly, "I ain't exactly an Arrow Collar ad, am I?"

He saved me an answer—I didn't have one, anyway—and quickly added, deeply serious, "Now you keep these drawings you been making of me all together, feller, and some day I'll put in a bid for them."

He lowered the drawing; then, as if our roles were reversed—Carl the artist now—he peered into my face with half-closed eyes so the details of its present contours would fall away, and my face of ten years ago would then be revealed. "That face!" he said, shaking his head. "When I first met you, it was a lot thinner and darker, and you needed a shave even after you'd just had one. Right away it struck me: he looks like an Italian Chicago gangster." Then he boomed out a laugh, slapped me on the shoulder consolingly, and added: "but a gangster with a heart of gold, because you play the guitar."

Then he rolled his eyes, and I could see that he was making ready to roll a few vowels around on his tongue and play them on his vocal cords. He particularly luxuriated in the Latin lushness of the voweled and syllabic structure of my name. "Gregorio d'Alez-z-z-z-io," he chanted sonorously, like the opening line of an oratorio. Then softly and almost reverently he added, "d'Alez-z-z-z-io for president!"

When Sandburg nominated you for the presidency, there was no question for all time that you were his pal. It was never proposed mockingly or patronizingly, only in pure affection and fun. You knew early in the game whether you were making it with Sandburg; and you knew soon enough if he liked you or not. He might let you know with a look or with a silence, without hem or haw, heckle or hector, chevy or chivvy.

Sandburg liked to play around with my baroque, Italianate surname in another way besides putting it into the air and trying out its sonic nuances on the acoustics at hand. He also liked to write it for variations of its spelling. That is how I prefer to interpret what was probably a simple doubt on his part as to its spelling each time he had to write it. But as many times as he spelled it incorrectly, he also spelled it correctly. Once, however, he not only spelled it incorrectly, but gave it a totally unexpected variation.

On a late Wednesday afternoon of an early spring day in 1957, I returned home after having made the rounds of the magazine and newspaper cartoon editors scattered over the town. It was a discouraging day; out of a batch of some seventy-five roughs I'd shown to ten or more jaded, dyspeptic editors, there were a mere three "holds"— not sales—but "for further consideration." Remembering the reluctance with which the editors set the few roughs aside, I knew that I might as well have stayed at home and painted a picture or something which no editor would have to judge. I plopped myself down before my large drawing table and gazed blankly at its surface, clean but for a scrap of paper up at its corner, near the phone. On it was scrawled something immediately recognizable as Sandburg's distinctive handwriting. He had left it there, no doubt, after having made his phone calls for the day. I brought the flimsy bit of paper up close. Scribbled at the top of it was a series of squiggles I had earlier drawn, trying out a ball-point pen, and then left there on the table. Now, at the bottom, was written "Carl d'Allessio." He had thrown in an extra "l." But I thought it was still the most precious piece of writing he could ever leave behind for me. The spelling may have been wrong, but the spell was right; it restored me, and I knew that on the following Wednesday, I would again face my sour-faced editors with new stuff and new hope. Now Sandburg had dubbed himself, part of my "family." I liked that more than I did being his president.

On a blustery, cold day in early March 1957 Carl Sandburg and I rounded the corner of Eighty-sixth Street and entered our alley after an invigorating walk. It was already March, but in Henderson Place we were getting that extra bite of cold, that frostier quality of wind which characterizes deep mid-January weather, and which the city beyond had seen the last of weeks earlier.

Newspapers and other windborne refuse swirled about testily and finally settled down, trapped under parked cars or caught by a railing.

Dutifully, I policed the street, picked up each unwelcome piece of windsam, crumpled it into a tight ball, and dropped it into the nearest rubbish can—one whose cover was missing, lifted earlier by a strong gust. There it was—the lid lying in the middle of the road, waiting for another ride on the wind. I restored it. I recovered other lids and recovered more tightly the other cans which had blown their tops.

Sandburg, whom I had left at our door, was standing on the top step. I realized with dismay that I should have let him in out of the cold before starting out on my manicuring duties. He seemed unperturbed, however, and he regarded me with a surface soberness, underneath which, if I know him, he was thinking how funny it all was—this fastidious, conscientious bustling about, putting my street in order.

Now a car appeared at the head of Henderson Place. Slowly it advanced, suggesting stealth rather than the caution required to negotiate the tight squeeze, clearly intending, my experienced eye told me, to squat into a parking space vacant of its legitimate owner. I approached the skulking driver, pointed vigorously to the PRIVATE STREET—NO PARKING sign plainly visible, and ordered him off the premises. Surprisingly, he backed out and left.

Up toward the end of the street, smack in the middle of the road, I spied an abandoned tricycle standing perkily, and next to it, a junior bicycle lying flat. They belonged to the Jaeger kids of Number 14. I lugged both cycles over to the protection of the Jaeger doorway.

My work finished, I finally got over to Number 8, where Carl was still waiting patiently, watching me all the time as I went about my compulsive chores.

The next morning, Carl descended from his flat to make his daily batch of phone calls at my drawing table. Before slipping into the waiting chair, he bowed ceremoniously and handed me a slip of paper about 4″ x 9″ in size, covered with his simple, open handwriting, in pencil. He said, "This well-deserved citation was wrote special for you." He handed it to me with a flourish. I read:

> *Whereas Gregory d'Alessio has by his intelligent concern with duties related to the cleanliness and outward appearance and inner aspects of the various premises of Henderson Place*
>
> *And whereas G. d'A has with industry, zeal and rare skill devoted himself to various tasks requisite to the symmetry and utility of our community, be it hereby Resolved, that we designate G. d'A as The Man of the Year.*
>
> *Anno Domini 1957*
>
> *Carl Sandburg*

This nomination, even from so influential and eminent a figure as Carl Sandburg, somehow never came to the attention of the editors of *Time*. That year, Nikita Khrushchev made their cover.

The Poet Gets a Haircut

SANDBURG WAS HOISTING a spoonful of minestrone, and he lowered his head to meet it halfway. Two locks of creamy white hair tumbled forward from his temples and dangled before his eyes, barely clearing the soup as it made its way upward to mouth. Slowly, he lowered the spoon back into the bowl, removed his glasses, pushed the springy white forelocks back, and pressed them against his ears. Carefully, he replaced his glasses, bringing the stems firmly across the unruly locks, pinioning them like wings against his temples. He addressed himself again to Terry's soup without further interruption, and in final tribute to the culinary genius of the Missus, he tipped his plate toward her in courtly salute and scooped up the last minuscule of the minestrone. Straightening up, he wiped his mouth with a napkin and asked, "Where can a feller get a haircut around here?"

Carl Sandburg was no longhair poet; but sometimes, he was a poet with long hair—a matter of postponing a trip to the barber's for one reason or another, not the least of which was economical. Carl was a poet with crystal clear vision. He knew that the time was nearing for a shearing when his hair got so close to his soup bowl.

Between the two great American poets Carl Sandburg and Robert Frost, similar in looks, close together in age, but worlds apart in poetic vision and style, there existed a definite respect. Sandburg's regard for

Frost's art was open, Frost's for Sandburg, grudging. Frost took a cool view of Carl's openhearted friendliness, his folksy humor and simplicity, his personal appeal, dramatic looks and delivery of song and poetry on concert stages across the country, and especially those flopping and flying white wings of hair. Once he aired his opinion of the famous hair, saying that he suspected that Carl *liked*—indeed affected—that hair falling into his eyes.

"The closest barber shop is Mario's, just up the street," I answered Carl. "He opened up only a few months ago, and I go there all the time."

"Just up the street," Carl repeated. Then he shook his head. "Too close, too close."

Too close. Now, I wondered, what was wrong with that? I said, "There's one I used to go to before Mario opened up his shop here. It's along Third Avenue around Eighty-eighth or Eighty-ninth Street, Bauer's Fancy Tonsorial Parlor. Bauer seems old enough to be one of Yorkville's earliest settlers."

"Any others farther away from that?" Carl asked, and he winked mischievously, giving away his game. Though his hair was growing longer by the minute, a haircut would only be incidental to a walk— as long a walk as possible and with the usual Sandburg trimmings: uphill, against the wind, and today, in a powdery swirl of snow.

"None that I know of farther than Bauer's," I lied. There were plenty of barber shops at greater distances, but Bauer's was as far as I could possibly endure the weather conditions of the day. I knew Sandburg would invite me along, but before he could I essayed a cop-out. "Now you just walk to Third Avenue, turn right, and somewhere between Eighty-eighth and Eighty-ninth, on the east side of the street, you'll find Bauer's. Have a nice haircut."

Carl cut me off. "You're going with me," he said firmly. He always cited the great physical benefits of walking. Pointing to my thickening middle, he grinned, "You can lose some of that," and pointing to my thinning hair, "and some of that."

"We get haricuts together," I said resignedly.

Sandburg's subject for today was hair. "You can't help feelin' closer to a town after you've had a haircut in it," he said. "The towns I remember best are the ones where I left hair behind."

"Every time I go to a barber's," I said gloomily, "the price of a haircut has gone up."

"Maybe we oughta go to one of those barber colleges down in the Bowery where they give you a bargain haircut just so they can practice on you."

We had walked a full block, and now we were passing Mario's. "There's that new barber shop I told you about, Carl," I said. I added, "Wouldn't you like to give it a try?" My question got caught up in a swizzle of snowflakes before it got to Carl's ears.

"This feller Bauer," he queried. "The usual talkative barber type, is he?"

"Yes, and in thick Yorkville accents, too," I answered. "Bauer still has a cabinet of private shaving mugs with his old neighborhood customers' names on them," I recalled. "You'll see. We're almost there now."

"Does he have a customer named Wolfgang Amadeus Himmelgerstenfarber?" Carl asked. "Then his name would meet itself comin' round the other side, or the mug could be next to another saying CONTINUED ON MUG #2. Say, there's a cartoon for you!" He stopped walking and talking, and looked up. "Here we are—Bauer's Fancy Tonsorial Parlor," he said reading from the ancient, flaking gold-leaf lettering on the window before us. On its lower right-hand corner— did I see it or did I imagine it—I saw the ghost of a long-vanished line of lettering reading CUPPING ALSO DONE.

Like all barbers waiting for customers, Mr. Bauer sat near his window, viewing the passing show. He sat in his Number One chair, white-coated, white-haired, calm, inscrutable, as if one customer more or less, or no customers, was all the same to him. When we entered, he rose slowly and grunted a greeting. From an excess of outdoor cold, we were now almost smothered by an excess of heat from the battered old gas range gasping in a corner.

Bauer was short and portly. I knew from experience that Carl and I would be in for a stomach-bumping when Herr Bauer pressed closer to perform some nuance of his tonsorial technique, particularly behind the ears.

"You first," I said to Carl.

"No," he said gallantly. "You first. Age before beauty." He laughed; I laughed; Bauer glowered. He peered sharply at Carl through his thick, steel-rimmed specs, and I thought, Well, that tears it; he's recognized America's great poet-historian (in that year, a frequent guest and panelist on TV shows). Now we're in for a lot of fussing around, maybe neighbors called in for a look-see at a genuine celebrity getting a haircut at Bauer's, of all places. Then a mad scramble for locks of Sandburg's celebrated white hair among the sweepings, or maybe even before it was cut away from his head!

But as one old man to another, Bauer addressed Carl, "You are maybe a neighbor? You are new around here?"

Carl simply answered, "Uh-huh, uh-huh," as Bauer beckoned me to his Number Two chair.

In less than fifteen minutes, the silence broken only by the continuous wheeze of the heater, the snip-snip of scissors, the soft thud of stomach bump, and finally the scraping of razor around ears, Bauer stepped back like a painter from his easel, the better to survey his finished masterpiece.

"Donnick?" he asked.

"No. Just a dash of witch hazel and water," I answered, looking down at the hair that had accumulated on the floor beneath my chair, puzzled for a moment as to whose hair it was for its startling grayness. Surely some old man had sat in my chair earlier for a Herr Bauer haircut, and all those shearings around me had yet to be cleared away.

"Neggst," Bauer said, and Sandburg promptly rose, making for the Number Two chair I'd just vacated. But Bauer waved him to chair Number One, bowing stiffly from his long-lost waist in Teutonic fashion. Did I hear a faint click of heels?

"There iss a bedder light by the findow," he explained. Although he did not know Sandburg from any other white-haired contemporary, he must have felt a certain Number Oneness about the poet, and naturally assigned him to chair Number One.

Carl climbed smoothly into it, like a king ascending a throne. Indeed, sitting in the barber chair with all that red plush around him, he looked like a white-crowned legendary Viking king. With the grace of an overweight torero executing a *paso de pecho,* Bauer waved the coverall sheet and secured it at Sandburg's neck. Above its white swathings, Carl's face beamed like a disembodied sun.

"How do you like for me to cut the hair?" Herr Bauer asked, scissors poised.

Sandburg circled a finger around his white thatch. "Just a general clippin'," he said. And the snipping began, counterpointing typical aimless barber-to-customer talk. Carl was never patronizing; in fact, he was surprisingly as dull as Bauer. They were two old gents who could have been sitting in front of the general store, whittling and passing the time of day swapping yarns, none of which would be remembered or even heard by the other.

The shop was now overwhelmingly hot. Over my copy of an old *Life,* I began to perspire, as much from apprehension about the old gas stove as from the heat it emitted. Its dangerously unvented, all-orange flame sputtered noisily, consuming any oxygen left in the air. Atop the range, a kettle steamed as a feeble gesture toward relieving the parched air. Let's get out of here before the explosion or before we pass out, I thought in panic. Let Bauer speed up that haircut! By the time he finished, Sandburg would need another one!

Bauer was having trouble with some unruly tufts of hair at the back of Sandburg's head. Comb and hand pressure had not worked; the hair sprang up again. Finally, Bauer fished around in a drawer and brought up a straight razor, whose handle, I saw, was not plastic, but old-fashioned bone. With a comb between scalp and razor, he began to carve away at the stubborn stubs. Modern barbers call this process a razor-cut, or a contour haircut, but this was no amusing anachronism in an ancient barber shop. It was pure and simple necessity. Bauer chose the tool, and he solved his difficulty; he didn't know a contour haircut from a lobotomy. But the business with the razor impressed Carl.

"Say, that's all right," he said admiringly. "First time I ever got this kind of a haircut."

Bauer restored the razor, picked up the scissors again, and with geometric accuracy, shortened Carl's forelocks to just above the eyebrows. The *haircut* was over; now came the crowning touch, the *combing.* With the precision of a surgeon making his first incision, Bauer lifted the point of the comb, and immaculately parted the hair off center, just above Carl's right eye. Bauer stepped back, cocked his head, and eyed his master stroke critically.

Satisfied, he proceeded to his next step. Carefully, he combed out both locks smoothly, sideways and down, so they rested on the forehead, just as they did when Carl had first sat in the chair—an arrangement which Bauer must have wondered about, but perhaps had dismissed as the carelessness of an old man, or the effects of the wind outside. At that point, I made ready to go; perhaps we'd still make it before the gas range exploded. Carl's hair was as combed as it would ever be, or as it had always been. But as far as Bauer was concerned, there was yet the third step—the coup de grace.

With a flip of comb and wrist, he swept each wing up from Sandburg's temple, and with the guidance of his free hand, brought it to the back of the head. There the locks rested, but only for a moment. Slowly, rebelliously, they rose, threatening to snap back to their familiar places at Carl's forehead. Bauer, a simple haircutter, seemed puzzled. He was not aware that in ordinary hair, the chief chemical property of the threadlike filament is a horny substance called keratin; or that in Carl's hair, nature had added another ingredient: tempered steel. The hair continued to rise above the body of the shorter hair underneath. Again Bauer attacked. This time with the aid of a shot of tacky tonic, the hair stayed, tamed and obedient. It looked like a glossy piece of marble sculpture. It gleamed; Bauer beamed; Sandburg beamed; the kettle steamed, and so did I.

For minutes, the three of us were frozen into a tableau of suspended animation. Carl cool, Bauer proud, myself in shock. Sitting there with his forehead exposed, his hair in a fine pompadour reaching almost to his occipital, Carl looked the respectable banker— a benevolent one, to be sure, from whom you could get a loan without security because he liked your face. Only once before had I seen Sandburg's noble brow, but only for a split second. Several years before, on a TV panel show that included Beatrice Lillie, the mischievous British comedienne impulsively leaned across to Carl, and with both hands, pushed the white forelocks up and away from his forehead. "I've always wanted to see how you look this way," she giggled. But this was a TV first that the viewer would have missed had he blinked once. Carl lifted his hand in a good-natured gesture of protest, and Miss Lillie quickly let go of the hair. The locks sprang back like released springs, and an alert percussionist in the orchestra off camera produced a synchronized "boinnng."

Now, sitting regally in the chair, hair groomed beautifully, his ruddiness inflamed by the heat of the shop, Carl looked illustrated, like a Leyendecker ad of the twenties. Bauer picked up a hand mirror and held it at the back of Sandburg's head for the final okay.

"Good, good," Sandburg nodded. He gestured toward Bauer's breast pocket. "Would you mind lending me your comb?" he asked ingenuously. Bauer gave the comb a few quick wipes and handed it to Sandburg. He nodded his head; he understood. The customer always likes to take the last few licks at his locks after a combing by a barber, and though he might not approve of such tampering with his creative coif, his professional pride was not too much hurt.

Sandburg brought the comb up to the part in his neatly slicked-back hair. With a quick downward movement of his wrist, he flipped over one wing. Eagerly, it sprang to rest at its old home against Carl's forehead. He repeated the operation with the other. Now he looked much as he did when he had first entered the shop, less whatever hair lay on the floor at the base of the chair. Herr Bauer waited calmly. What else could this be but the preparatory first step of a finicky customer, in a final revision of his work? But there was no second step. The elegant Bauer hair-do was back again to its original Sandburg hair-don't.

Carl handed the comb to Bauer. "Thank you," he said to the dazed little barber. Then he motioned for release from the coverall, stepped briskly down from the chair, and adjusted his tie before the mirror. His shortened locks bounced gaily with his every movement, as if in joy and celebration from their short exile to the snowy Siberia at the back of Sandburg's head.

"The haircuts are on me," Carl said. He extracted three crisp singles from his small leather pocketbook and handed them to Herr Bauer. "Keep the change," he said.

The bewildered barber muttered a low "Donka," found a broom in a corner and began slowly to gather together the accumulation of Sandburg-d'Alessio hair, bringing it to a mound of pearl gray. He pushed the sweepings into a dustpan, stepped on the lever of a nearby rusting refuse can, dumped in the hair, and released the lever. The lid dropped with a tinny bang.

As we left another customer entered. "Neggst," Bauer addressed him, looking sharply at his head when he removed his hat.

12

Play It Again, Greg

WORKING AWAY AT MY DRAWING BOARD one afternoon, I could catch the rise and fall of Sandburg's singing filtering its way down the stairs and into my studio. He was doing his daily half-hour of vocal calisthenics. The strains of his simple guitar accompaniment shyly asserted themselves between his phrasings. This was an exercise which Carl performed regularly, wherever he might be, whenever he could, even as he faithfully performed his favorite physical calisthenic: lifting a chair over his head many times a day. There were plenty of chairs of various sizes, shapes, and weights in his rooms for his physical exercise needs. For his daily singing exercises, I'd offered him my best guitar—only the best in the house for the guest in the house—but he quickly refused it.

"I wouldn't think of it," he said. "That's your best guitar—the one you always play—and it wouldn't be happy with me. Your second guitar, or even your third is good enough for how I play." Then he paused and smiled. "If you have a fourth guitar, that'll be good enough, too."

And there was a fifth and a sixth, even unto an eleventh guitar strewn about the house, all of them in different states of playability, not to mention two lutes, a theorbo, a mandolin, a violin, two ukuleles—and at one time, a five-string banjo.

There were nights at Henderson Place when neither Carl nor I was committed to any social obligation, and these memorable hours were spent among the guitars. Carl tried out those at hand, singing a song that had just come to mind, sinking deeper and deeper into his armchair, a shawl wrapped loosely around his shoulders, a blanket around his legs, down to his pigeon-toed feet. Taking time out from his two-fingered playing, he would reach for his two fingers of bourbon. He had been playing my number one guitar, and now he was handing it to me. And I knew what was coming. "Play 'Number Two,' Greg," he said.

When he let you talk, Sandburg was the world's best listener. When he let you play, he was even more attentive than that. Usually a player of "Music to Talk By," I was in the middle of my repertoire one evening, and in my glory, receiving undivided attention from Carl. I had played some Bach, Sor, Tárrega, Carcassi, and Giuliani. Now I was off on an arrangement of an old Mexican folk song by Manuel Ponce; it was the second in a suite of three such pieces whose melodies were on the lips of all Mexicans with the same familiarity as "Down in the Valley" was to Americans across the border.

"What do you call that?" Carl asked.

"I don't know its exact Mexican title. I always call it 'Number Two'."

Carl said "Play it again, Greg." On my number one guitar, I played "Number Two" again and again and again into the night. That was how "Number Two" became number one on Carl's hit parade of guitar pieces.

My steady playing of the Mexican song at Sandburg's nightly urgings turned me into a virtuoso performer of that particular piece. The enforced practice not only strengthened my fingers in the right places, but more important, it gave them memory. With each playing of the song, I cleared away a smoother path to its end, interpreting it with more subtlety and giving it more nuance, even venturing to invent a rubato, imparting to the song a distinctive cachet of my very own. Although it was I who played the song so often, it became Carl's song.

I always felt that although Sandburg had long before given up hopes of becoming a skilled instrumentalist, "Number Two" was one piece he could have played had he tried.

As Carl's visits to Henderson Place began to dwindle, my skill with

"Number Two" faded. Now, with Carl gone since 1967, I cannot even play the opening bars. My fingers have lost their memory. Without Carl listening, the song will not tell my fingers where to go. Nothing like that song brings Carl back to me, so deep is my desire to play it; but it not only eludes me, it resists me. It refuses to be played without Carl present, sitting there, sunk into the armchair, stogie and bourbon lifted in alternating turns to his mouth, and for the umpteenth time saying, "Play it again, Greg."

Carl's great pleasure was two-part singing, and it always delighted him when he found a kindred spirit. I liked it almost as much as he did, and we did a lot of it together. If Van and Schenck were still hot in the vaudeville circuits, they would do well to look to their laurels, said Carl.

He had a good enough ear for harmony, if a given song did not call for hauling too close to the wind. But the songs we sang were simple, their harmonic tracks hardly ever varying from tonic, to dominant, to sub-dominant, and back to tonic. Sandburg's voice was magnificent, musical, and always on pitch. He was a good marksman.

Sitting around trying to remember harmonizable songs, I soon realized that while Sandburg was the Father of the Folk Song, he also liked popular songs enormously, no matter how banal the lyrics or mouldy the music. He would often come up with a tin pan alley pop song whose lyric was a typical inanity of the day, and sing it down to its last June or moon, kiss or bliss, love or dove. It was strange to hear, coming from the lips of a poet of taste and sensitivity, a master craftsman of English rhetoric. Indeed, at the core of all his works is a pure lyricism. He sang out the trite, cliché-rich Woolworth pearls of great price innocently, merrily, without scorn or ridicule or mockery. He was simply going along with the taste of the people of the moment, not as a lofty, patronizing observer, but as one of the people.

The two A.M. hush of a weekday wrapped up the city like it was in a sleeping bag. Sounds of traffic, people, pigeons, planes, dogs, and other urban fauna had long receded and were now at their lowest ebb. Within our house, the silence was broken only by the lingering bong of the clock striking two, the last strains of song and guitar, and the sigh of the furnace at the thermostat's command to retire for the night. Sandburg, too, had just retired. Now I was locking up.

Nine times—count 'em—nine times, I had played "Number Two" for Carl during our music-making, and as I became sleepier and sleepier, openly nodding, he grew wider and wider awake, eager to keep the music going. Why, like any other man his age, or even men much younger, did he never once fall into sudden sleep in his chair? Finally, with my ninth playing of his favorite and my long yawn which followed it, Carl took the hint, and folded his tent for the night.

But there was another break in the silence, one which startled us out of sleep. The phone rang, and with it, echoes of a tragedy of more than thirty years before.

It was a bit after two A.M., March 15, 1958. From the phone at my bedside came a high-pitched voice, thin and reedy, almost a whine: "This is Nathan Leopold. I am at Idlewild, between planes. I'm on my way to Puerto Rico, and I understand I can find Carl Sandburg there. I apologize for calling at so late an hour, but it's the only time I have. If Mr. Sandburg is there, will you call him to the phone?"

Nathan Leopold. Of course! The newspapers for the past few days had been carrying stories about his impending release from prison. And now I was hearing his voice, the legendary, almost forgotten co-murderer of the boy Bobby Franks in Chicago at least three decades before this night. Whining, gentle, disarming, the voice of this once demon-possessed man filtered its way from the distant airport. It sounded disembodied, other-wordly, certainly much farther away than Idlewild, and I thought melodramatically that he was calling from his lonely cell in Joliet Prison through lines secretly opened for him by an underground criminal organization. But in its stark reality, it was the plaintive voice of a weary soul redeemed at last to start another life. Leopold could not leave without thanking Carl, who had been so nobly instrumental in securing that chance at redemption.

I must say that speaking to a thrill-murderer made me react with moral revulsion when I thought of the heinous crime which Leopold had helped commit with his collaborator, Richard Loeb. I wasn't overcome with compassion for this convicted murderer, young as he was when he did his violence. It did not matter how much sadder and wiser a man he might be now, presumably deeply remorseful of his sin.

I was overcome with a protective concern for my guitar pal and the consequences of his sticking his neck out in a hazardous situation. Suppose that, restored to society through the generous intervention of

Sandburg and other distinguished public figures who spoke up for him, Leopold betrayed that trust and reverted to type? What if the long-slumbering seeds of some smoldering, congenitally antisocial nature burst forth again into ugly bloom? If the grisly murder which he had helped perpetrate in 1924 when he was nineteen was some kind of a cathartic episode in his life, then maybe, now in his mid-fifties, the worst had not been seen yet. Was it wise that Carl Sandburg, big-hearted and compassionate, but no psychologist or sociologist, take a chance at being responsible, even at the very least, for such a horrible aftermath, no matter how remote its possibility? Carl had spoken on behalf of Nathan Leopold a few days ago, before the Illinois Parole Board. I hoped he would not some day have to eat his words.

I had the wild idea to take it upon myself to edit out the phone call entirely—void it—telling Leopold that he was mistaken; that Sandburg was not here. But I thought, "Here I go again with my gratuitous over-solicitude on what is Sandburg's own business."

What an arrogation; I was his host, his guitar pal—not his mentor. Of course I would have to get Carl to the phone. I shook away my anxiety and asked Leopold to hang on. Carl was still awake reading and came down to take the call on my studio phone. When I heard his low, husky hello through my extension, I quietly settled receiver to cradle. But through my still-open door, I could hear the Sandburg voice, just the voice, not any of the words it made, but the music of its rise and fall and gesture into the still air. Never before had I caught in it such a coloration. Reassuringly, calmingly, comfortingly, Carl was talking to Leopold as to one just awakened from a nightmare.

Of course, the story of Nathan Leopold's farewell to Joliet and his departure to Puerto Rico, the isle of his regeneration, made all the papers the next day. Specially mentioned was Leopold's call in the night to Sandburg and Sandburg's statements to the Illinois Parole Board on behalf of Leopold. He had urged them to perform an historic act. After thirty-three years of exemplary behavior, the man should be freed. It was Loeb who'd masterminded the crime, and Leopold had meekly followed the "master." Loeb had been stabbed to death some ten years before in the prison shower room. Answering critics, Carl had said, "Those who perhaps won't like it are those who believe in revenge. They are the human stuff of which mobs are made. They are passion ridden."

As for the impact of his act on youngsters near the ages of Loeb and Leopold when they committed the crime—eighteen and nineteen respectively—Sandburg answered: "There has been a struggle toward light that any teen-ager could contemplate with healthy results."

All the next day, up to the hour when we settled ourselves with our guitars in the living room, I withheld comment on the call from Leopold, the newspaper accounts of his release, and my fears over the repercussions of Carl's intervention on Leopold's behalf. I was bursting to warn him, even to scold him for sticking his neck out so far. Little by little, as we played and sang and sipped the Jack Daniels, these apprehensions and misgivings all came out. Carl threw a worried look my way.

"You oughtn'ta get so worked up about it, boy," he said soothingly. "It'll come out all right—you wait and see."

The world and I waited for thirteen years, and saw a stunning regeneration, so complete, so total as to border upon sainthood.

Upon his arrival in San Juan, Puerto Rico, Nathan Leopold, kidnapper, thrill murderer, for thirty-three years shut off from society, quietly and voluntarily entered into another kind of confinement. He was a prisoner of his conscience, atoning by paying back his debt to society. He kept faith with those such as Carl Sandburg who had taken a chance on giving him another chance. He immersed himself in selfless deeds, going to work as a lab assistant in a church medical mission at ten dollars a month, throwing himself zealously into the social, educational, welfare, and health problems of the island. He taught mathematics, studied leprosy, aided the poor, all in a ceaseless effort to atone for the crime that lay corrosively at the center of his consciousness. On August 30, 1971, Leopold was suddenly released from his self-incarceration. He died of a heart attack. He was sixty-six, an age divisible by eleven.

"It'll come out all right," Sandburg had said calmly, confidently, that March night in 1958. He dismissed the matter, gesturing with his cigar stump toward the guitar I had rested against the side of my chair. He settled himself serenely into his listening position, deep in his chair. From his cocoon of scarves, shawls, and comforters, came his last words of the night.

" 'Number Two,' " he said huskily. "Play it again, Greg."

Carl and the Campfire Girls

FROM THE MID-FORTIES on through the fifties, I was a card-carrying member of the Camp Fire Girls.

I had to join. My wife, a resolute guardian of a group of Camp Fire, Blue Birds, and Horizon Club Girls, dragooned me into service.

The Missus had all three age groups. And where did they camp, these Camp Fire Girls? Why, where else but at our house? The Missus was den mother, of course. I was den father. As an added bonus to the already over-privileged little dears, they also had a den grandfather: Carl Sandburg.

They were all over the place. I tripped over them constantly. I found them, feet up, two or three at a time—in my favorite armchair. They were always in the bathroom. Without notice, I was pressed into service by my wife as their official guitar accompanist in the songs they sang, chants for which I groped around my guitar for chords nowhere found in the lexicon of music. They went through their rituals, sitting in the middle of the living room around a frighteningly realistic-looking campfire made with red paper over a hot bulb which threatened momentarily to flare into the real thing.

They were especially in evidence when Carl Sandburg was on the premises. My wife saw to that. She sent out smoke signals to all her papooses when he was expected. In no time, they would miraculously appear. Kids were for him; he was for them. His attitude was totally unlike my testy desperation when in their midst. He was kindly and entertaining, and was in turn entertained. He had lots of rewarding, grandfatherly fun with them. What a story *they* would tell their teachers and schoolmates the next day!

But these sudden stories were not all romp and happenstance. The girls finally sobered up, climbed down off Sandburg's shawled knees, and were soon immersed in a serious project which Terry had been preparing for them. It was to be a gift from the Camp Fire Girls to Sandburg. Their assignment: in short, episodic phrases, each girl was to tell the story of Abraham Lincoln in Indian symbols, from his humble birth to his premature death, the whole to be fashioned into a collection of scrolls and presented to Carl Sandburg at a future Camp Fire ceremony.

There were eleven separate scrolls, one by each girl. The story emerged in childlike simplicity, bright and clear:

1. *A flower is born, touched by the star of destiny.*
2. *Growing years like birds flying toward the sun.*
3. *Thoughts and speech are his weapons.*
4. *He is chosen center figure of head council of all states of the nation.*
5. *Ominous signs and rumbling over the land.*
6. *The nation is divided by a dark cloud.*
7. *Lincoln presides as war chief over the solid north against those that would pull away.*
8. *Peace. Freedom is victor.*
9. *Slaves are released.*
10. *The Chief is shot by masked player in place of entertainment.*
11. *He who stood tall in the center of nation's council flies with wings of Eternity. His name shall live forever.*

At the council fire ceremony of Terry's Rainbow-on-the-Horizon group, the scrolls were presented to Carl. First there was the traditional candle-lighting ceremony, then the singing of the Camp Fire song "Wo He Lo" (Work, Health, Love). The shaky guitar accompaniment was provided, of course, by Great White Den Father. Then the girls, all in buckskin fringes, headbands, and beads, solemnly offered the scrolls to Carl Sandburg. He was deeply touched and he accepted them with great dignity.

"Thank you," he said. "I will treasure these."

Then he added: "Work, health, love—the world could use a lot of that—especially the last named."

Another year, another group of girls, another Sandburg visit to Henderson Place, and Terry, still heady with the success of the Lincoln scrolls, hatched another idea for a special gift to Carl from her fired-up Camp Fire Girls. This time the gift would be something more personal to Carl. Since his visit had been announced on short notice, and was to be a brief one, only a single hastily called meeting of the girls could be convened. It was decided that the effort would have to be one, cooperative crash project. Eleven girls comprised the group. Together, they pored over the pages of Sandburg's *Complete Poems,* looking for an eleven-liner. They found a suitable one at last in *The People, Yes.* Then each girl took a single line as her assignment, to be translated into Indian symbols, cutting out patterns in various colors after having first decided on the *motif juste.* Finally, the pieces were affixed to a length of moss-green felt in their proper sequence as the poem dictated. The poem reads:

1. *The sea has fish for every man.*
2. *Every blade of grass has its share of dew.*
3. *The longest day must have its end.*
4. *Man's life?*
5. *A candle in the wind.*
6. *hoar frost on the stone*
7. *Nothing more certain than death,*
8. *and nothing more uncertain than the hour.*
9. *Men live like birds together in the wood;*
10. *When the time comes each takes his flight.*
11. *As wave follows wave, so new men take old men's places.*

Upon completion, the eleven lines fell into an overall design which had the *shape* of a poem, a result not present in the prose put together by the girls in making up the Lincoln scrolls. As a design of arresting visual aspect, the Lincoln prose did not come off. Carl's poetry, however, lost nothing in visual translation.

Sandburg turned the scroll this way and that, inspected it closely, marveling at how his free verse had been transmuted from word into picture, retaining its symmetry and order and reflecting the free flow of his poetic thought. He was pleased, nodding his head vigorously, his lick of creamy white hair bobbing up and down in counterpoint.

"Uh huh, uh huh," he said. "And so is a syllable distillable into a simple symbol."

In a letter to me a few weeks later, Sandburg wrote, "Please tell Terry her Indian sign keepsakes are treasured."

All during his long life of writing, when asked from time to time to discuss his poetry, Sandburg answered: "I reached for pictorial words as the Indians and Chinese have them."

Knowing nothing of this, the Camp Fire Girls and their guardian, my wife, in an effort to honor him the best way they could, had stumbled naturally upon his professed poetic technique.

He searched for pictures and made them into words; they found his words and made them back into pictures.

Sandburg on Art

CARL SANDBURG AND I weren't *always* playing the guitar, or singing, or partying, or gallivanting about or celebrating something; we also celebrated, as when we sat and talked about art—his, mine, and other arts. Thus we met on our professional levels. On his, I was the rapt listener; on mine, I was still the rapt listener. Sandburg's thoughts, ideas, opinions, and insights on any subject always made fascinating pictures.

He never discussed poetry with me analytically. He simply read it. Fishing into a remote inner pocket, he'd bring out a crumpled typescript, saying, "This one hasn't been published yet, and I'd like to try it out on you." Then, adjusting his glasses, his green visor, and taking a swig of bourbon and a drag off his cheroot, he'd read his poetry, as no one else could.

When we moved into the visual arts, painting, drawing, and sculpture, Sandburg's monologue would usually be triggered by the sight of a reproduction of a work of art as he idly turned the pages of one of the many oversized art books I had around the house.

Sandburg had the keen natural response of the poet's instinct; he could spot a fraud a mile away. He looked for the life force of a work, whether abstract or realistic, classical or modern.

If I thought that Sandburg forgot about our informal discussions when he left for Flat Rock after a visit, I was set straight soon enough. One day, I received in the mail a two-page carbon copy of a manuscript. It was in the large, familiar typeface of an old typewriter Carl was still using, and I assumed that it was an as yet unpublished piece. I had never seen it in print anywhere, nor had I read it or anything about it in a bibliography of his works. It was a set of eleven definitions of art—"experimental" as he termed them—but which were, in fact, another of his poetic forms. They bowled me over with insights about art that he had never verbalized in our discussions. In "experimenting" with definitions of art, Carl was neither defining, in the pedantic sense, nor was he writing about art in its glass case. He soared with it—wrote about it on the wing.

ART: EXPERIMENTAL DEFINITIONS
by Carl Sandburg

Art is an added touch that takes up life where animal necessity leaves off—it begins with the first dance, drawing, song, prayer, or luminous jest above the human subsistence line.

Art is the musical score of a smooth hush with a little wind whimper across it and then the hush again.

Art is the use by man of his impressions of the world outside and inside of him in the best imitation he can give of his heroes, clowns, and grotesques.

Art is the creative operation of a series of accumulated performances.

Art is an involvement of the questions: What is worth looking at? What is worth listening to? What do we live for? What is worth dying for?

Art is the vapor of mist giving up the ghost on a piece of silk in the sun.

Art is a signatured communion of dreaming bones.

Art is a devotion to numbers modified by a belief there may be spheres where two and two make five.

Art is the presentation of an onion in a manner not so strictly representative that people say: This is a real onion—but rather so the onion seems to be walking on stilts or coming down to earth in a parachute or dissolving in a mist of the atmospheric spirit of onions acquainted with soil that says, I have laughed with billions of onions and I am not yet done with onions.

Art is a commodity production aimed at customers who buy, also an offering of lonely men whose last thought is what buyers might want.

Art is a final performance beginning sometimes with a rehearsal rule: the first thing you do is break all the rules.

Cartoons

CARL LIKED THE WORD *cartoon*. It was a word in his style; he could play with it and make things out of its syllables. *Cartoon* stands out among other words. When Sandburg said *cartoon,* he oozed it out in a low maroon croon. Three of his favorite words could be made out of its seven letters: *car*—the box variety, of course; *art*—a vital word in English or any other language, and *tune,* which he never gave out as a refined t-you-n. It was always "toon" to him.

Sandburg liked cartoons so much, he once cartooned a poem. Like an idea for a cartoon, it began in his head. Then the hand went to work putting it down, not limned on drawing paper in pen and India ink, but hand-written or tapped out on note paper. "Cartoon," the poem is simply called; I found it in his *Cornhuskers* (1918). It is short and to the point, just like a cartoon should be:

> *I am making a Cartoon of a woman. She is the People. She is the great Dirty Mother.*
>
> *And many children hang on her apron, crawl at her feet, snuggle at her breasts.*

Sandburg could have become a cartoonist, if he had so decided early enough in life. Certainly, he had what is every bit of fifty percent of the good cartoonist's gift: ideas. He could have learned how to draw credibly. Sandburg's handwriting was calligraphic, and he knew how to design and compose for the space he was covering. His poems often began as pictographs in his head, and many of his examples on the understanding, the evanescence, the meaning of poetry have been drawn from visual artists. His favorite was Hokusai, the great Japanese painter, draftsman, and woodblock designer of the eighteenth and nineteenth centuries, who died at age eighty-nine, as Sandburg did. Other giants in the visual arts—the protean Picasso, the mystical Turner, the poetic Inness—also served Sandburg well in his attempts to explain the inexplicable in art—its vagaries, contradictions, imponderables, paradoxes, its timelessness.

Sandburg also liked cartoonists; he was a friend of many, most of them editorial cartoonists. Sandburg at a drawing board would not have turned out a comic strip or a panel cartoon, à la *The New Yorker,* though those forms of the cartoon art often delighted him. His high ideals, his humanity, his fierce intolerance of national and global "nincompoopery" called for the keen ax of editorial cartooning. That's how his graphic ideas would run. There are hints of that in other poems, such as this one:

HALSTED STREET CAR
Come you, cartoonists,
Hang on a strap with me here
At seven o'clock in the morning
On a Halstead street car.

> *Take your pencils*
> *And draw these faces.*

Try with your pencils for these crooked faces,
That pig-sticker in one corner—his mouth—
That overall factory girl—her loose cheeks.

> *Find for your pencils*
> *A way to mark your memory*
> *Of tired empty faces.*

> *After their night's sleep,*
> *In the moist dawn,*
> *And cool daybreak,*
> > *Faces*
> *Tired of wishes,*
> *Empty of dreams.*

(Chicago Poems, 1916)

101

That was Sandburg's "assignment" to a cartoonist—a big order, if not an impossible one; for a poem is a poem, and a cartoon, each an entity, even if the poem is about a cartoon or the cartoon about a poem. An inspiration does not come to an artist by way of the inspiration of another artist. Thus, Sandburg, a passenger on the Halsted streetcar of an early Chicago morning, was not seized with the urge to draw a picture, but to write a poem about drawing a picture.

It was in the course of my one and only formal interview of Sandburg that he said, "I like the word *cartoon*. If I were dying and had the choice of words among 'painting,' 'etching,' or 'cartoon,' I would choose to die with the word 'cartoon' in the air."

In 1957, cartoonist Alfred Andriola, creator of *Kerry Drake* and editor of "The Cartoonist!," official organ of The National Cartoonists Society, learned that Carl Sandburg was my house guest. He assigned me to ask the author of *The People, Yes* if cartoonists and their cartoons were included among the people he so emphatically affirmed in his poem. After my notes and quotes were put together, editor Andriola entitled my piece, " 'Cartoons? Yes!' Says Carl Sandburg."

Dominant sounds set the character of Henderson Place in those days: finger-plucked guitar strings, the sizzling of garlic kernels in hot, splattering olive oil, and the busy pencil whisperings and urgent pen scratchings of two cartoonists, the Missus and I, hunched over our drawing boards, feverishly bucking syndicate deadlines. Seeing us, Carl allowed as how he liked the sounds of cartoons in the making as much as the sound of the word itself.

Sandburg picked up a newspaper; the news and editorials, the printed words, were his first interest. He never turned eagerly to the comics for Mary Worth's latest meddling good deed in saving a marriage, or Batman's in saving the nation. "There are many things in life that I'd like to have as part of my life, but they take time," he said almost apologetically. "Why do some people turn anxiously to the comic strips? I've asked them; they say 'Well, I've got the habit.' "

But addict or no, Carl's judgment of a comic was canny and keen. Carl especially enjoyed *Peanuts,* the wry and rueful adult comic in the guise of a kid strip. Carl had been watching *Peanuts* long before it caught on.

"If I ever look special for a comic at all," he said, "I guess it's gotta be *Peanuts*." Coincidentally, as I prepared *Old Troubadour* for press, this cartoon ran in my daily paper! Charles Schulz never knew that Sandburg was a fan of his strip and had no idea *Peanuts* was even mentioned in *Old Troubadour*. The creator of *Peanuts* graciously permitted the use of this cartoon. I'm sure that Carl would have loved it.

He was honest enough to say this even though his host, interviewer, guitar pal, walking companion, guitar-toter, singing and drinking partner d'Alessio drew the cartoon panel *These Women* for the *New York Post,* a paper he read in those late 1950s for its liberal leanings.

Clearly, my cartoon was not one of his favorites; in all frankness, it wasn't mine either. It didn't even run a close second to my favorite, *Peanuts*.

"There's something about *Peanuts,*" Carl went on, "that reminds me of *Krazy Kat.* I used to read *Krazy Kat* regularly, and I had it in mind years ago that I'd like to look in on George Herriman sometime, to see what kind of a man he was. But then I thought, 'Hell, he can't tell me any more than it says right there in his work.' "

Sandburg admired several editorial cartoonists, including the mighty Thomas Nast, the Tammany Tiger slayer, the tweaker and twitter of Tweed, boss of bosses in the city of New York in the mid-nineteenth century. Daniel Fitzpatrick was Carl's good friend and a cartoonist of conviction and commitment to the cause of labor and liberalism, an artist in the Daumier tradition. Carl liked C. D. Batchelor and his symbol of war, not the stereotyped armorclad Mars, but a slinky prostitute with a death's-head of bleached blond hair. Another favorite was Herblock, who had his own figure of atomic war in the shape of a mighty bomb, bearing the brutal features of a low-browed, blue-jowled, cigar-chomping beer baron in an early gangster movie. Then there was Rollin Kirby and his gaunt, um-brella-totin' Undertaker, symbolizing Prohibition; and Bill Mauldin, the kid who once drew Willie and Joe, the sad, patient, ironical GIs of WWII, and then successor to the great Fitzpatrick over at the *St. Louis Post-Dispatch.*

Carl reflected on editorial cartooning and its symbols of instant recognition: "I remember the caricatures of Teddy Roosevelt—T.R., he was always labeled—his piano-key teeth and his Rough Rider hat. And speakin' of hats, nowadays you don't see that square, shallow hat made of newsprint, and wearin' it, the stocky, sturdy figure of a man with a terrific five o'clock shadow—Labor! I think I've grown tired of those New Year's Day cartoons that show the New Year as a baby and Father Time and his scythe saying farewell; they have become rather hackneyed symbols in cartoons. I'm glad to see the old figure of Mars representing war on the way out. I like C. D.'s and Herblock's; but the man of war these days can also be that silly-looking, ridiculous figure—the man with a briefcase, specs, and bald head—the Profes-sor!"

"The Professor?" I asked, a little puzzled.

"I mean the little feller in his laboratory with his formulas and equations, experimentin' with newer and deadlier bombs and chemi-cals; and the other feller at the drawing board, designing newer and deadlier war machines."

He had more to say on cartoon symbols and labels: "Then there's the anxious-looking feller, representing the Peeee-pull, or John Q. Public; or sometimes known as . . . ," Sandburg shot his lips forward to form his famous "ooooo" sound, and he boooooomed it out ". . . the Con-soooomer! He has a majesty and a terror about him. He is the author of revoloooootions! If I had time, I would make a collection of cartoonists' representations of him. I did a book *The People, Yes* that shows this feller as very meek, humble, helpless; and I mention the times when he's terrific, overwhelming—when he's both the irresistible force and the immovable object!"

I asked Carl what cartoon in all his years of newspaper reading and study was his favorite. Was it a political theme, or war, or poverty, labor, social comment, disease? Curiously enough, the cartoon he quickly chose did not deal with those deep subjects but with what struck at the very core of the black side of the human condition: Greed. He began to describe the cartoon. I remembered seeing reprints of the cartoon, but only vaguely could I put its parts together or evoke its mood. I was willing to bet that for dramatic and emotional impact, Carl's verbal cartoon would pack more power than its graphic counterpart.

"The cartoon appeared the day after the sinking of the Titanic sometime in April 1912. It's a stark and icy night scene in the North Atlantic. The mighty Titanic, steaming toward New York on its maiden voyage from England, trying to break all speed records for the everlasting glory and profit of the board of directors and stockholders of the White Star Line, has struck an iceberg. Lifeboats are all around getting out of the way, and many heads are bobbing amidst the floating ice—over 1,500 lives lost. And in the center of the cartoon, only the tip end of the ship is showing, about to take its death plunge into the black, icy waters, and it bears the word—," here, Sandburg paused; then, in a hoarse, barely audible whisper, he breathed out, "UNSINKABLE!"

Next the old Social Democrat and former labor reporter asked me a question.

"You say the cartoonists are organized now?"

"Yes," I answered, "but not along the lines of a labor union—striking, collective bargaining, and all that; and not like a social club, either. We have a code of ethics which publishers and newspaper syndicates are acquainted with and go along with—most of them anyway." I told Sandburg about the history of The National Cartoonists Society, which had started in the late 1940s with a mere handful, and then, in 1957, included 375 professional cartoonists with the legendary Rube Goldberg as its honorary president.

"Good, good," Sandburg said, nodding his head slowly, thoughtfully. "I'm glad to hear it. I like to see people who are in the same line of work get together in some kind of organization or society, in fellowship, discussing their craft, seeing each other's faces now and then." Then he began to chuckle softly. "When I was a boy in Galesburg," he said, "I had a job sweeping the floor and emptying the spittoons in a large real estate office. If, at that time, there'd been an Amalgamated Floor Sweepers and Spittoon Cleaners of North America, I would have joined it if only to occasionally look upon the faces of other floor sweepers and spittoon cleaners. I hereby salute the cartoonists of America and the keen harpoonery of their cartoonery!"

If Carl had ever happened to be in the steady company of people who wove Panama hats under water, very soon he would have become involved in some way with that unique and fascinating art, not as a passive observer, but as an eager helper; he would have wanted to make a hat; or he'd have suggested ideas for hats; or tried on the hats; if nothing else, he would have written a poem about hats.

Now Carl was living with two cartoonists in a cartoon factory, and here there was a frenzy of weaving ideas into pictures, bucking deadlines, producing reams of roughs for magazine cartoons, mailing material to out-of-town editors, visiting New York editors, and drawing, drawing all the time. Sandburg was at home in such an atmosphere, which reminded him of the hectic city room of his old *Chicago Daily News* days. Here in our cartoon factory, he was not content to be the mere observer. He stuck his nose into my business—not as the artist, of course—but as critic, idea man, judge, editor. And he shone at it; he was canny, alert, sharp, modern, perspicacious, and best of all, jollier than my weary professional editors peering skeptically at my weekly offerings, and wanly holding aside one out of the twenty—if I was lucky—"for further consideration."

It was when Sandburg came down from his upstairs quarters to make or receive calls at my drawing table phone that his interest in my labors became more than cursory. I was usually drawing, and Carl often caught me deep in my weekly production of cartoon roughs for the magazines—such as *The New Yorker*. He was always eager to inspect every new batch of roughs before I took them on their rounds along Magazine Row.

"May I?" he asked one day, pointing to the twenty roughs that lay strewn about my table.

"Be my guest," I answered. "Be my pre-editor, in fact. Tomorrow is 'look' day—when the magazine cartoon editors 'receive.' Why don't you look the roughs over, pick out the ones you think'll go, and see how your choices compare with the cartoon editors' tomorrow. Be as tough as you like."

Carefully, he scrutinized each one, putting each cartoon in one of two piles. He went through the twenty, taking at least fivefold the time the morrow's editors would give them. Finally he picked up the roughs he'd placed on his right, four out of twenty.

"I like these fine as they are," he said. "I'd like a few others if you could clear up a thing or two in them." Eagerly, I riffled through the rejects and pulled out the three which Carl indicated to me as needing doctoring. Swiftly, I made the changes to his satisfaction: a facial expression here; a verbal expression there, in the caption; the addition of necessary detail somewhere else.

My score the next day: the four editors I visited had held out, among them, seven of the twenty roughs in the batch for the final art conference to be held further along in the week. When the final answers came, the first "holds," the three whose clearing up Sandburg had suggested, had been so improved as to get quick O.K.'s. The four others were held for further consideration and sold the following week. They were major sales, too, at top money. Sandburg, shining knight in green visor, stuck his nose in my business one day and batted 1,000.

Flushed with his success as a cartoon editor, Sandburg now moved in as a writer, throwing ideas at me daily, all of them of sufficient substance and professional caliber. They were worth the time it would take to make a rough and submit it to an editor. Actually, Sandburg did not write a single line; he gave his ideas to me orally and with appropriate gestures, beginning with: "How's this for one of those *New Yorker*-type cartoons?" When I had a dozen of his ideas, I went to work on the roughs, putting together what I called my "Sandburg batch." They made a great showing on the magazine rounds; in time, they all sold. Sandburg had batted a thousand again.

There was also a thirteenth idea—ill-fated, of course, to preserve the inflated reputation of that pesky, hard-luck number. It got to my drawing board, all right, but never off it. Sandburg unfolded his idea to me: "This feller is being ushered into a jail cell by a guard, to begin a stretch." He stopped a moment, frowning. "Now how're we gonna show it's a stiff sentence he'd gotten? I guess you'll be able to do that by showing him as the type who couldn't commit a petty crime—a habitual criminal. He's a rugged character, with a busted nose, big jaw, and needin' a shave. As he enters his cell, there is an ecstatic, almost beatific expression on his face, and he's stretching his arms back lazily and deliciously, saying, 'Ah! Now to learn the classic guitar!' " As Sandburg spoke, his face had taken on the bliss of his character, and he acted out the gestures of his jailbird with loving accuracy. He *was* the jailbird. He slapped his knee and hawed. "I guess you know who the rugged gent could also be."

"You, of course," I quickly answered. "But didn't you once say that one of the five things you want out of life was to keep *out* of jail?"

"I did say that, didn't I?" he nodded. "But at one time, I wanted to learn to play the guitar in the classic style so bad that I couldn't think of any other way to find the time to do it except by doing time."

Sandburg had once done time. When he was a teen-ager, he was clapped in a county calaboose near Pittsburgh for freight-hopping. Ten dollars or ten days, the judge rapped out. There was nothing like ten dollars—or perhaps even ten cents—mingled with Sandburg's pocketful of youthful dreams, so the would-be knight of the road chose jail for the ten days.

The idea, conceived by Sandburg, written by him, acted out by him, was now on my drawing table ready for its metamorphosis into the cartoon idiom. Carl had also described his jailbird; but that, I felt, was redundant if not gratuitous, for the character was one of the best known in the central casting department of my mind—a dependable, instantly recognized stereotype. I started to draw him. To my dismay, I found I could only conjure up a dull, colorless, static figure. I called upon him to act, but could not get the performance out of him that Sandburg had gotten out of himself. Nothing else would do. Then, almost as if the hand were remembering, and not the brain, I found myself drawing Sandburg himself entering the cell, an ecstatic, almost beatific expression on his face, stretching his arms back lazily and deliciously, saying, "Ah! Now to learn the classic guitar!"

Thus, the "Sandburg batch" missed being a baker's dozen. I had drawn something that was no longer a commercial cartoon. Instead, it had developed into a fond, personal memoir—one of my meager, precious store of "Sandburg Papers"—something you don't put in the funny papers.

The Artist
and His Model

CARL SANDBURG WAS A SOUND MAN. He was also a sound-man, not in the technical sense of recording sounds, but in making them. He played syllables and words against each other until some sillysally Rootabagatelle came out. Not all of his wordplay was sheer nonsense. If you dug deeply, you would often find relevance, satire, and bite.

Of the many sounds he toyed with, Sandburg seemed to be mostly under the spell of OG. OO was another sound which often reverberated in his writings. But it is the OG which merrily jogs through three of the best known poems in the entire body of Sandburg's works. Who does not know of the *"Fog* that comes in on little cat's feet"? Or the "Chicago" poem that begins *"Hog* butcher of the world"? But my favorite lines along that line are these from "Bitter Summer Thoughts":

> *This here phizzog*
> *somebody handed it to you—am I right?*
> *Somebody said, "here's yours, now go see*
> *what you can do with it."*

The phizzog poem is my favorite, because phizzogs are my business. I have been drawing faces since Kaiser Wilhelm's spiked helmet and spike mustache fascinated me as a kid during WWI. I have drawn thousands of celebrities, but the one I have drawn most often is Carl Sandburg. His phizzog dominates my sketchbooks. I began drawing him when he was seventy. My last sketch of him— from life, that is—is dated 1963. His presence wasn't necessary; I could draw him whenever I wanted to. I have done dozens of drawings from memory. Once I cracked the secrets of his face, it was easy.

As phizzogs go, Carl Sandburg's was well endowed. Carl's face had interesting form and color, and his characteristic Scandinavian bone structure remained intact from his maturity until very close to the end of his life. At least, in the years I knew and saw him, and even in photos of him that go back to the twenties, there seemed little if any change in the contours of his remarkable phizzog. Indeed, as the years passed, he always looked the same to me. His hair seemed no whiter or sparser; his figure showed not an ounce of weight variation; his movements appeared no slower, though I doubt if he ever moved swiftly much after his basketball days at college. When he stood on his feet, he was virtually immobile; he never wasted motion. Mrs. Sandburg told Harry Golden that when standing, Carl would lean forward slightly, like a fast-ball pitcher winding up and pulling the string on a batter. That's right. Her mentioning it brings up a correct picture of him. But sometimes, standing there, thus poised, with toes slightly turned in, a mischievous twinkle would light up his eyes. Suddenly he'd fling out a leg, loose and surprisingly limber; his foot dangling freely, he'd strike the wooden floor with two quick slaps of his toe, in the manner of a vaudeville tap dancer.

If Carl had a suit of clothes other than his blue serge, I don't think I ever saw him in it. Certainly his wardrobe must have included other colors, weaves, or models. When in New York, which was when I saw him, he would frequently be invited to some exciting affair, function, or dinner that called for black tie. Here, the blue serge was most serviceable. All that was required was a change of shirt from the loud woolen plaid he usually knocked around in and equally loud tie, to a white shirt and black tie—which was often not even black, but of a dark color and sometimes with a pattern.

He was an unforgettable study, and I drew him in quick gesture style many times from life. Later, this image became so deeply engraved on my vision and imprinted on my brain that I could draw him from memory with ease—carrying or playing the guitar, writing, phoning, just sitting or standing. His unstylish dark blue felt hat was also a familiar part of the silhouette, a hat that, on a chair or a rack, looked drab and undistinguished, but on his head became a masterpiece, a dramatic accent on him.

Sitting, he made an excellent subject. Conscious of posing or not, he seldom moved, because extraneous movements were not his way—except, of course, for the movement of his arms in writing, smoking, playing the guitar, drinking, and eating. His gestures while talking were negligible. He never punctuated the air with his hands. His torso was granite-still. Against any chill in the air, he covered his legs with a shawl. Around his neck and back he wrapped a scarf, always a part of him, indoors and out.

In sharp contrast to the calm and repose of his body was the great mobility of his face. I was fascinated by the activity of the line of his eye sockets and what was visible of his forehead, hidden as it was by those white forelocks, and enthralled by the narrowing and widening of his small frosty blue eyes, setting into motion a myriad of creases that radiated like a sunburst from their corners, clear out to his ears. Like a trident, three deep creases were etched into the space between his brows, a design formed over the years from frowns of thought rather than from grimace or ill humor.

"You're drawing Sandburg? He ought to be easy with that white hair and all," said an undiscerning friend of mine. The hair is some help, of course, but it is not part of the essence of his facial structure, constant though his white thatch remained over the years. To prove that point, I even tried a portrait sketch of Sandburg, concentrating on the design of his white hair against his pink face, but glossing over the bone and muscle significance of his features, the gesture of the face in all its component parts. I failed. The hair and the coloring were superficialities. Understanding the skull—that's the problem. The portrait artist and the caricaturist, particularly the latter, who knocks out a drawing in a minute, is concerned with not *how* his subject looks, but *why* he looks the way he does. What is the one characteristic that establishes over every other characteristic of the face the "why" of a person's looks? Find that, and you have solved the face. Get every other detail pinned down but fail to get the "why" and you strike out. Miss everything else by a mile, but manage to pinpoint that one salient feature, and you'll get a base on balls, at least.

After much study, I finally discovered the "why" of Carl Sandburg's face. It was his mouth—especially the area which the skull
chart identifies in scientific terms as the superior maxillary bone over
which are spread the zygomatic muscles, or, in everyday language, the
upper lip. In the case of Sandburg, "superior" is most apt. As upper
lips go, it was ample, a typically Scandinavian facial characteristic;
and because of its generous proportions somehow I always felt that it
cried for a mustache. With such a distraction, however, it would not
have been possible to appreciate the acrobatics of that remarkable
mouth—how it took shapes that were just right for certain words he
spat out. How I loved to see him form a big "O" with his mouth, and
then hear him roar the hated "ex-clooooosive." Sometimes he curled
his lips with scorn and in a higher-pitched, flatter voice, rapped out:
"obscura-a-a-antist." There were more pleasant words like "keeeeen"
or "goooood." They flowed from him like a blessing. They were as
much a part of his physical image as the sonic image that fell on the
ear. They went together.

Sandburg could speak no other way. It was natural. The instrument which fashioned the sounds and made them issue forth sonorously was simply built that way, just as the cello, the organ, the guitar
are built. So was Sandburg his own sound box. Some people thought
this verbal delivery was affected or too juicily overtoned, but whether
he was addressing Congress, speaking on television, or simply con-
versing at the breakfast table with one or two other people, the same
buccinator and zygomatic muscles of his Scandinavian face went into
action—and the same music came out.

There was an environmental factor which could not help but affect
his speech inflections. His parents were Swedish. Virtually from the
cradle and on through his years at home in Galesburg, Illinois, the
Swedish-accented English, and the actual Swedish lingo always in the
air must have penetrated deeply into the boy's consciousness. Thus, he
could not help but speak English with the musical forms and syllabic
emphasis of the Swedish language, with its sharp rises and falls and its
prevalence of the sound made by 'O' or 'OOO.' Go to an Ingmar
Bergman movie and see what I mean.

Archibald MacLeish liked the way Sandburg pronounced Peoria.
Phonetically, as he pointed out, ordinary people say "Pe-AW-ria." As
MacLeish faithfully demonstrated in his moving speech at the poet's

memorial services in Washington, Sandburg pronounced it "Pe-OH-ria."

Consider Carl Sandburg's phizzog: if you drew a line straight down from Sandburg's stubby nose, you found that his chin retreated within the boundary made by that line. For a skull with so little chin, Sandburg's face was nevertheless remarkably strong, the thrust of the entire maxillary area presenting the profoundly personal expression of the man. This is what the patient portrait artist looks for, not the superficial adornments, but the basic facts of the immutable bones.

Though Sandburg made enough television appearances in his lifetime to qualify for several AFTRA cards, he could not exactly be termed an instantly recognizable public figure. Some of our more attentive citizens did recognize him on the street, in restaurants and theatres, but most did not. However, he unfailingly took one's attention; all gazed at him puzzled—they could not help it—he was a commanding figure. They felt he must be *somebody,* this tall, picturesque, humorously visaged, white-haired gentleman, in blue serge most of the time, his hat dark and floppy, but not too eccentric, even for a poet. Around his neck some kind of scarf was arrayed so intricately that you wondered what the combination was for undoing it? His bow ties, distinctively and originally knotted, were masterpieces of sartorial nonchalance, defying imitation (I know; I tried).

When understood and extracted by the artist, a subject's gestures do not necessarily connote violent movement or quick impulsive action. They have more profound meanings, as much spiritual as physical. A person's movement, his own unique way of standing or sitting, make for recognition as much as physical features do. Gesture, in this sense, means knowing somebody instantly even from a distance or in a fog, knowing him by the way he carries himself, by a movement of the body peculiarly his own without the need to make out any of the actual details of the body. This, the artist or any discerning person cannot help but learn to do in time, especially when he is close to his subject and gets to know him better and better. Here again, he has discovered another "why"—the "why" of movement— or lack of movement. In seeing so sharply and expressing so beautifully that stance of Carl's as "leaning forward like a fast-ball pitcher winding up and pulling the string on the batter," Mrs. Sandburg extracted his gesture with pinpoint accuracy.

It is rare that the face of a poet becomes so well known to millions as Sandburg's features did. But Carl's features deserve more lasting preservation than the memory of a television image or even the countless excellent photographs taken of him by dozens of photographers, including the best of them all, Edward Steichen. His face should be carved into another Mt. Rushmore by a gutsier Borglum, even at the cost of replacing an image already so graven. In that event, I would eliminate Theodore Roosevelt (the least successful artistically; that toothy grin is sorely missing) and assign Carl's phizzog to that spot.

Then he would be next to his beloved Abraham Lincoln.

The Silly Center Opera Company

DURING CARL SANDBURG'S extended stays at Henderson Place, there were parties galore. I hasten to say that these exuberant festivities were scheduled with strict deference to, and at the discretion of, our distinguished guest: whether Carl felt physically up to them; whether he was in the mood; whether he was concerned over the exigencies of his work program.

He always felt physically up to them; he was always in the mood; and his work always got done, somehow.

No, if there was any restraint toward the frequency of parties, it was feebly expressed by me.

It was I who couldn't keep up with the pace. But once the parties got going, I forgot my cautious concern for moderation. I valued the joy more. These gatherings where Sandburg sat among us like a mischievous old uncle were memorable still.

Ever since that day in 1948 when Carl unabashedly set out to track down the guitar people in New York, he was one of us. It had always been hard enough keeping our sans-Sandburg parties small, but when word got around that the poet-troubadour was to be in our midst, it was impossible to avoid a scene here like the last night of the Mardi Gras in Rio de Janeiro.

A few years earlier, I would have gnawed my nails in worry over the imposition of such frenetic festive activity about the white head of my old friend; but I'd learned to spare my anxieties. Sandburg could take care of himself. It became evident that he even preferred the more-the-merrier type of party as long as there was no ebb of bourbon and the guitar was always in earshot.

When I arrive at a party, I listen automatically for the reassuring, comfortable sound of the guitar. Hearing none, I look about for the instrument. When I find myself trapped at a guitarless party, I realize how much I depend on the instrument as a buffer from bores—an old friend, a shield against stilted, inane chatter with strangers.

I draw a line on parties where there is no guitar music awaiting me.

Our first party at Henderson Place started out as big and unwieldy. The crescendo of noise finally reached the ears of our neighbors and next the attention of the police. Two big officers appeared at our door at the height of the high jinks and issued a firm but polite warning to pipe down lest even our overworked Mayor Wagner, himself fast asleep over at nearby Gracie Mansion, be robbed of his precious rest.

Although the party got so completely out of hand, there was never a trace of vulgarity, drunkenness or roughhouse—just high spirits and a level of noise unavoidably high with so great a crush of guests milling about.

During the height of the festivities there came a call from a neighbor whose sleep was being disturbed. Carl blew a cloud of cheroot smoke at the phone and said, "That feller who just phoned: somebody oughta tell him that some laughter is better than slumber."

Clearly, though, if there were to be more parties, and if the guitar were to be paid its proper homage, our enormous guest list called for a drastic slashing.

During the festivities Carl had taken the measure of the guests, evidently forming his preferences. Planning our next party, we found to our relief and delight that we could leave the problem of a curtailed invitation list entirely to him.

"Ethel Smith? Dolores Wilson?" I was reading from a new list I'd made.

"Yes, yes," Carl said decisively. "And don't forget Olga Coelho," he added.

This intimate photograph is streaked with shadows, but my memory of this boxcar afternoon remains as clear as the ringing strings on our two guitars. We were at my Tudor City apartment with William Arthur Smith, fine artist with brush, camera lens, and engraving tool. The U.S. Postal Service commissioned him to cut a Carl Sandburg Commemorative which was issued in 1973. He also was behind the shutter on this day in October 1952.

" *... papa's in the jailhouse ...* "

Carl won me over when the first song I ever heard him sing was a quatrain in which the melodrama of life and death is played out in *fourteen* words, to a basic blues melody.

$\mathcal{S}$andburg waxed pensive, with a guitar built by Domingo Esteso resting on his lap, while Leonard Steckler took this picture at Henderson Place on July 19, 1959. The night before, Carl and Edward Steichen had opened "The Family of Man" exhibit at the Museum of Modern Art. One day later they took it on a worldwide tour, with Russia as the first stop.

TWO-TAP DANCER

Standing there poised, with toes turned slightly inward, a mischievous twinkle would illumine his eyes. Suddenly he'd fling out a leg, loose and surprisingly limber; his foot dangling freely, he'd strike the wooden floor with two quick taps of his shoe.

"AH! NOW TO LEARN THE CLASSIC GUITAR!"

*S*andburg confessed, "If I were to land in jail sometime, it would be a good chance to learn the classic guitar." My cartoon produced a deep, sonorous guffaw when I showed it to him.

"EXCL O-O-O-O-SIVE!"

Carl's perennial answer to the question, "What word do you most hate in the English language?"

carl Sandburg
at 314 E 41st NY
april 20 1952

*C*arl's cheroot was ever-present. I drew this on April 20, 1952.

During his sojourns at Henderson Place, Carl was summoned to the telephone so often, I felt obliged to exercise a prudent amount of editing of his calls. "Oh," he said, waving his stump of a cheroot around in an expansive gesture, "Let 'em come—let 'em come. I want to take them all."

"Right—Olga Coelho; and what about Kitty McCarthy, John Cosgrove, Eileen Lange, Len and Olga Steckler? Eric Ericson?" I submitted more names.

"Uh huh, uhhuh." Carl nodded in agreement. "And Joe and Shirley Wershba, Virginia Pasley, and that small cartoonist, Irwin Hasen. Sure, sure!" he continued. "Invite them all; they're family, you know. They're family!"

These were some of the people Sandburg favored. Most of them were musical. Several played guitar. The rest were happy just to be listeners. Altogether, it was a congenial, well-knit group—a "stock company" which included not only the players, but just as important, a built-in audience.

On a typical evening the performances did not start until a huge platter of the Missus's paella and many flagons of sangria were consumed.

Warmed, mellow, and oiled, voices of different timbres, textures, and colors began, one by one, to punctuate the air, rising slowly and blending finally into a swelling chorus. Each vocalist sang with direction and great assurance.

But what were they singing? No known piece of music, that was sure.

It was a meandering path the music traveled, to no apparent resolution. Anticlimax followed anticlimax. When it seemed the last chord was at last struck, one of the singers, maverick fashion, would take flight on a cadenza of his own, and again a new ending was in the making.

Barely had the last strain of the impromptu overture faded away when, during the slight pause that followed, the same idea struck each member of the company: an opera had begun. The artists had no inkling or plan of what it was to be or where it would go, but endowed with fits of parody and mimicry, they boldly raised the curtain on the opera with a typical *recitativo* between frail soprano-ingenue and cocky hero-tenor.

The soprano was always played by diminutive Ethel Smith, who started out in life as an organist, then developed into a fine guitarist, singer, and actress. Though her professional singing with guitar was devoted almost entirely to comedy songs, her voice was once rated good enough to essay the role of Anina the maid in a Salmaggi production of *Traviata*. Violetta's maid, the pathetic fallen woman of

117

La Traviata, is a role calling for great expressions of sorrow and concern for her dying mistress; but Ethel's comedy sense refused to stand aside. She could not help infusing her performance with a subtle, tongue-in-cheek comic-compassion.

Our hero was cartoonist Irwin Hasen, also diminutive, but far from frail; he was stocky and robust, the archetype of the old-time, pre-diet Italian tenor. His voice was loud and clear. His performances in the tradition of the Italian bel canto were gems of satire. He was a master at reproducing languages which sounded so like the real thing, even a master of a particular tongue would have to think twice before he was sure that what he'd just heard sung so spontaneously and authoritatively was pure gibberish.

After several exchanges of lively *recitativo,* as if on a pinpoint cue from careful rehearsing, came the aria between the two sweethearts—hysterical protestations of undying devotion to each other, accompanied by every cliché of voice acrobatics and flamboyant gestures known to old-fashioned opera. Now they were doing *La Boheme;* then, *Traviata,* or *Lucia,* or *Manon.*

Enter now the female heavy, Dolores Wilson, beautiful, blond, buxom, and a bona fide Metropolitan Opera star. Possessing a wide range, her voice could travel from a thrilling coloratura soprano to a menacing dramatic contralto. One of the best actresses on the opera stage, Dolores satirized with gusto and vehemence her contempt for the simpering heroine and her scorn for the fatuous fool of a hero. Sometimes she sang snatches from actual operas, but smoothly, flexibly, with scarcely any notice of a sudden turn in the "plot," she easily swerved into abstract vocalizing—marking time until the next line of development was tacitly communicated by mental telepathy.

An ominous knock on the door, and Ethel Smith became La Traviata again. She squeaked out a consumptive "Avanti!" and boldly, our barrel-chested baritone, John Cosgrove, strode with ponderous mock-dignity to center stage. Assuming a stiff nineteenth-century stance, he became the elder Germont, father of Violetta's lover, Hasen-Alfredo. Soberly, in pidgin Italian, he launched into a near-version of the denunciation aria from the second act of the opera as Violetta clutched at her ravaged bosom.

Then, as the last sad and rueful bars of Germont's aria faded away, there came ringing throughout the house a long, high-pitched voice, as from a cavern on a distant shore of a strange and mythical sea.

It was Siegfried! Closer and louder came the voice, and into the room lumbered big Eric Ericson, our Melchior, our golden helden-tenor. The mood suddenly changed. From an airy vibrato Verdi, we made a quick detour into weighty Wagner Weltschmerz, and the air filled with guttural Teutonic double-sing.

Len Steckler, silent and patiently waiting in the wings for a cue, any kind of a cue, would leap forward. He was an instant Brünnhilde. Though his masculinity was beyond doubt, his castrato-soprano made you wonder; it was pure, unstrained, and of remarkable power and clarity, and he conjured up all of the outrageous, overblown interpretations of the noble, nubile Norsewoman of the Nibelungen Ring.

Throughout the operas, I was the orchestra at the guitar, doing my best to follow the lines of music—sometimes actually establishing the lines, and cueing the singers into their parts with chord introductions, which, if nothing else, suggested the key and perhaps the tempo and mood.

Our opera fantasy exploded spontaneously on the night of our first "family" party with Carl Sandburg. Finally the singers exhausted their voices and ideas. Sandburg, hugely delighted but more amazed at such a feat of consistent, protracted improvisation, rose from his deep chair and in true claque enthusiasm applauded, calling out: "Bravo, bravo!" Then he raised his hand, waved it ceremoniously over the heads of the players, and said tremulously, with deep reverence: "You are a group, outstanding and astounding. I dub you now The Silly Center Opera Company."

The noise, excitement, and cheering that characterized our operas, wherein both cast and listeners were participants, had the gay festive air of a corrida. The guitar had a lot to do with that—its character, its timbre, its very *Spanishness*. *Olé* after *olé* rang throughout the house and well into the precincts of Henderson Place. Sandburg alone sat back calmly, periodically puffing at his cheroot, sipping his bourbon, and now and then chuckling low and deep at the shenanigans.

Some evenings were quieter, evocative of the dark, hushed interior of the old railroad boxcar.

"A boxcar evening," Carl called such sessions, and he, the hobo of yore, unwilling to suppress the memory of those days three decades in the past, was king.

119

In our guitar group, almost everyone could sing a little and play a little. Everyone knew at least one folk song he could sing and call his own. Nobody else, therefore, even if he felt he could do it better, would raid the repertoire of another. For instance, "Cool Water" was my song, and it was sacrosanct, though Len Steckler knew it perfectly and could sing rings around me. Thus, in a group of a dozen or more, the process of passing the guitar could go well into the night. By way of approbation, Carl would hail each singer with "Len Steckler for President!" or "D'alezzzzio for President!"

But when the guitar got to Carl Sandburg, he kept it for the rest of the time.

His repertoire was inexhaustible; his three-score-ten-plus memory for the lyrics of his songs was fantastic. In the relaxed atmosphere of his beloved boxcar, he sang on and on. This was not only his hour; it was his life. I sensed that nothing gave him more pleasure.

Sandburg's attention toward performers at parties was not only polite and respectful, but intense with keen personal involvement. He would so enjoy a song that he would importune the singer for reprise after reprise.

When Sandburg was center stage, he did not solicit your attention; all he insisted on was your silence—any kind—respectful, enraptured, intimidated even. Once in a while, nettled by some unwarranted but not deliberately rude interruption, Carl would abruptly stop playing, take a long and hard look sternly into the eyes of the quaking offender, be he famed actor, distinguished educator, celebrated author, or stylish psychoanalyst, curl his lip, and spit out a harsh and prolonged, "Shussssh!" On this touchy subject, Sandburg was frank: "If you don't care to listen and want to leave the hall," he once said about his singing, "it will be all right with me."

As long as Carl reigned over The Silly Center Opera Company, all of our gifts for improvisation were stimulated. But without his appreciative presence, we didn't have the heart for it. As for boxcar gatherings, there was even less chance of carrying these on without Carl.

Still glowing after our last "family" party, and feeling warm and sentimental toward each member, Sandburg wrote me: ". . . we seem to be a fraternity-sorority, a clan and a gang not needing oaths, passwords, or secret signals."

Up at Ethel's Place

ETHEL SMITH WAS AN EARLY MEMBER of The Society of the Classic Guitar. She always loved the instrument and played it expertly. She was also an organist, singer, comedienne, and actress on continuous tour with her quintuple-threat talent and winning personality. She was instant ingratiation onstage, be it in Hackensack or Hong Kong.

Offstage, Ethel Smith was no different. With my friend Carl Sandburg, when they first met at Henderson Place, it was instant infatuation.

In a career already studded with success, principally in films and in radio (the famed "Hit Parade" of the forties), Ethel's biggest success came in the film *Bathing Beauty,* with Esther Williams and Red Skelton, in which Ethel played on the organ that brilliant Brazilian samba, "Tico, Tico."

Her comedy songs and her skillful guitar accompaniment fascinated Sandburg and turned him into a fan. Her tiny frame was almost lost amidst the maze of keys, stops, and footbasses of the massive Hammond organ console in her apartment. But diminutive Ethel coaxed enchanting sounds from the pliant instrument.

"She's the Queen of the Organ, that's what she is," intoned loyal subject Sandburg after first hearing her in an impromptu recital at her home, playing Bach, Beethoven, Brahms, boogie-woogie—and of course, the piece always demanded—"Tico, Tico."

So it was natural that after a few days' stay at Henderson Place with no evidence of Ethel Smith among our many visitors, Carl stopped our music at an artistic height never before reached and inquired as to her whereabouts.

As if in answer, Ethel called, a day later, just returned from a Paris engagement.

It was more than a perfunctory call. She was in a dither of excitement: although Carl's eighty-first birthday on January sixth had passed while she was still abroad, she was anxious to give him a birthday party anyway. Belated or not, she was determined to make a tribute to Carl.

In Ethel Smith's sprawling half-acre apartment, parties were a natural phenomenon. The one planned for Carl Sandburg's birthday promised to be a bash of extraordinary size and brilliance, considering the guest of honor and his power of attraction.

While most of Ethel's friends were show folk, there were also artists, writers, newspapermen, and publishers. After a dinner party given for one group, a sizable quantity of stew might be left over. This promptly called for another party on the very next night with a totally different cast of friends, to consume the leftovers. One such party, which was a huge success, was built around some leftover cheese-cake—no ordinary cheesecake, however— but a creation bearing the distinguished hallmark of Lindy's restaurant, the house that *cheese-cake* built, with an assist by *lox* and *bagel*.

There were times when one or more strings would snap on Ethel's guitar; this was also a sure sign of an impending party. Changing strings was not only too complicated an operation for Ethel, manually and technically, but simply too time-consuming. Thus parties at Ethel's were very often been built around a sudden need for a guitar restringing; and at the spontaneously arranged soirees, there were sure to be some guests who would gallantly volunteer to take over the onerous job for their hostess. Like me, for instance; or on one occasion, Rodrigo Riera, the eminent Venezuelan concert guitarist and composer. He not only spent half a party making a complete change of strings on one of Ethel's best guitars, made by Hauser of Munich, but became so taken with the sweet mellow tone of the instrument that for the rest of the party, he played it without stop or regard as to who was listening. Though all of us were, you can bet.

When a guest arrives at most parties, he soon finds a drink in his hand. Not so at Ethel's. After your outer duds were taken by a maid, you'd move into the party area; there to greet you, instead of a drink, Ethel would plop a percussion instrument of some kind into your hand.

If there were fifty guests, she'd dredge out fifty implements from cupboards, cabinets, and shelves. These were Brazilian mostly, but also included Cuban, Spanish, African, Indian, Persian, Chinese, Japanese instruments and others of exotic origin.

Soon it became evident that the entertainment was on a do-it-yourself basis, with Ethel at the organ playing with one hand and conducting with the other. The crash of maracas, au-go-gos, bongo drums, cymbals, castanets, and other weapons of percussion would shake the very walls, floor, and ceiling of the apartment. Fortunately, Ethel's immediate neighbors, Conrad Nagel and Louis Sobol, were not at home. They were at Ethel's with percussion instruments in their hands.

On the night of Ethel's tribute to Carl Sandburg and his eighty-first birthday, all conversation was willingly dropped. I even forgot my chagrin and frustration over not getting to talk to June Havoc, whom I'd been worshipping for years. She looked ten times prettier in the flesh than on screen. There she sat serenely, only a few arms' lengths away from me, but alas, Ethel had assigned to me as my percussion instrument of the night the gourdlike raucous Brazilian reco-reco, which precluded my holding a drink, much less Miss Havoc's lovely hand.

A party of the size of this gala was a courageous undertaking. Any gathering in Ethel's apartment, with its view, terrace, and bar, was off to a good start. No expense was spared. The catering and supervising of the viands at the party were by Theodore himself, maitre d' of the Waldorf. The legendary Lucullus could not have produced a more fabulous feast for the fifty guests. Theodore surpassed himself when he unveiled a life-size bust of Sandburg, carved in ice by an anonymous but painstaking artist. The sculpture stood in a deep tray, swarming with clams and oysters. At hand was a dignified white-coated, white-gloved professional shucker to serve the many guests crowding around the gleaming sculpture and holding their hands out for more of the crustaceous delicacies.

Even without these gastronomical delights, Ethel Smith could still have pulled off an unforgettable evening. When she threw a big party, it bore a resemblance to a telethon benefit for the Heart Fund or Muscular Dystrophy. Money could not buy it. A giant talent herself, and adored by her friends, most of whom were likewise talented, she could organize a party brimming with celebrities and entertainment by a mere crook of her finger. A bash at Ethel's was always the talk of the town the next day.

This was especially true of Carl's birthday party.

Despite the ever-present danger of being pressed into service as a percussionist or as a more specialized performer, nobody stayed away from Ethel's parties: at bottom, everybody was really more than willing to contribute to the fun. With the legendary Sandburg, the problem was the Herculean one of trying to keep down the size of the crowd. The harried hostess was still apologizing to peeved, left-out friends well into the rest of the year 1959.

But the party went on, hurt feelings or no. It was spontaneous combustion; everyone seemed to arrive at the same time. There were no fashionable late arrivals or grand entrances, although the ladies were competitively and exquisitely gowned. All were anxious to pay homage to the old poet and exchange a few words with him, if the continuous entertainment permitted.

I made a panoramic sweep of the people, from face to face. Everywhere I looked, my eyes rested on a celebrity. Ethel was perched in her aerie at the organ, conducting a number; the guests were either listening or playing their instruments. Especially arresting was the sight of the stately actress Stella Adler wielding one maraca as if it were a scepter.

But if Carl spotted any celebrities on sight, I saw no such evidence. He was a simple country boy when it came to the Who's Who of the show business social register. Indeed, a famed Broadway and cinema star of those days actually had to introduce herself to the guest of honor. He didn't know her; but he did know her former husband, a writer, who was far from the public figure his glamorous wife was. Mention of the name brightened Carl's face quickly and he praised the writer's work to the actress ex-wife.

The audience participation entertainment soon came to a crashing finale. All of the comrades-at-percussion instruments had become firm friends in their common safari led by the determined Ethel Smith. Now it was the turn of the soloists; they were poised and anxious to entertain their fellow entertainers.

June Havoc was on first. She departed from the image of the frail blonde, lovely and languid—and launched into a lusty "Sam Hall"— the "God damn your eyes" refrain enunciated with all its hate-packed venom and anger. Miss Havoc, a fan of Carl Sandburg since her childhood, had reached into his *American Songbag* and pulled out "Sam Hall," a great favorite of his. She recited it to the hilt of her histrionic powers. When it was over, her eyes were brimming with real tears. So were Carl Sandburg's and everyone else's.

Brazilian singer Olga Coelho came prepared in every way. She'd brought her own guitar—and with it, an even better instrument: her magnificent voice. She sang her modinhas, fados, emboladas, and other Brazilian folk songs, especially "Meu Limon Meu Limoero," Sandburg's favorite, with a gusto and nostalgia that brought back to the sentimental poet the evening of his first meeting with Olga via her 78 recording of the song at Hazel Buchbinder's in Chicago back in 1938. Many other artists serenaded Carl that night.

But Carl Sandburg had not yet taken his turn. As Ethel told it later, like an old fire horse, he was champing at the bit. He was becoming apprehensive as the entertainment progressed toward its end, lest he be forgotten among the wealth and abundance of talent, and lose his chance to get off a few songs of his own before the party dissolved. From time to time, after each performance, Carl actually tugged at Ethel's sleeve, asking plaintively: "Now?"

Of course, Carl was not forgotten—not likely. Ethel was saving him for last; but next to last came Sam Levenson, a folksy entertainer in his own right, whose frame of reference was the world of his momma and poppa and family life in their New York Jewish ghetto. "A great American humorist," Carl called Levenson, "somewhat in the tradition of Bill Nye and Artemus Ward."

A hard man to follow, Levenson—but Carl Sandburg transcended the mores and customs—the superstitions, even the realities of show business. Ethel actually had a professional spot-lighting system rigged up in her living room for just such evenings of gala entertainment, and Carl sat in it at last, singing well into the night that he had inspired.

Carl wrote to Ethel soon after, "The memory of that party lingers with me absolutely—high as the sky and deep as the sea . . . your wings are invisible but you have qualities of an angel."

That was true—Ethel did have wings. I called her a few days after the party and asked how she was. "In the clouds," she answered. "In the clouds."

19

Miss Bankhead

APRIL 2, 1959, WAS A BIG DAY in the life of Tallulah Bankhead, Richard Boone, Nancy Kelly, Martin Gabel, Len Steckler, Olga Steckler, Virginia Pasley, Terry d'Alessio, a young man named Ted, a waiter at Sardi's, and your correspondent.

This night, Carl ever the guest in his travels, stepped out of that familiar role into a new one: he played host, and he played the role well—or at least with great originality. First, we ate dinner, seated around a special table at Sardi's. Dinner at Sardi's is in itself a heady start for a night on New York Town. But even headier events lay ahead. We were to take in a Broadway opening and visit a living legend whose identity our own living legend would not reveal until later.

After a convivial dinner, Carl gestured to the hovering waiter, moving his hand across the air as if he were writing. The small elderly waiter got the message, nodded, produced his book of checks and ripped off the top one. It had been ready and waiting. He laid it tenderly on the table in a spot next to Carl's elbow, face down. Carl picked it up, looked at it casually, and then, adjusting his glasses, gave the check a closer examination.

"Chees-us wept!" he said softly.

My peek at the check revealed it to be just under fifty dollars.

These were not 1930s Depression dollars, but modern, already inflated 1950s dollars. I knew the size of the check was not inconsistent with Carl's budget. He was in that stage of life an affluent, if not fairly rich, man, for a poet-troubadour. He could make money almost at will, constantly being sought after by recording companies, television networks, publishers, lecture bureaus, and other agencies who knew there was still gold in the old poet. There was no danger of a ruined evening washing dishes in the Sardi kitchen in order to pay the bill.

Carl reached into an inner pocket, pulled out five new ten-dollar bills and placed them on the check. The waiter whisked the package away. In a few minutes he returned with the change, just under a dollar, on a brown plastic tray, and put it before Carl with a ceremonious bow. And there it lay like a time bomb.

We all looked at it apprehensively. The waiter stalked the table, brushing away crumbs, but scrupulously avoided touching the tray. Clearly he was waiting to see some paper money placed upon the silver.

Carl rose. "We'd better be pushing along," he said. Then he looked down at the tray, picked it up, tilted its contents into his other hand, and pocketed the money.

"Oh, well, if they don't want it, it's all the same to me," he said.

The size of the check had surprised and nettled him. While it was not in the least beyond his purse, it was beyond his world.

I had expected to see an outraged waiter, untipped as he was. But he hardly seemed miffed. He simply shrugged his shoulders philosophically. He even smiled, watching us leave, and actually murmured polite good nights.

Len Steckler paused at the door. "I've gotta go to the john," he said, turning back into the dining area. The rest of us went through the swinging doors and waited outside. Len returned in a few minutes, and we began our walk to the theatre.

I dropped back a few steps, pulling Len with me. I said, "Through the window, I saw you talking to the waiter. What was that all about? Did he make a beef?"

"I stopped to give the waiter a tip. I made him take it."

"*Made* him take it? You mean he refused it at first?" I asked.

"Yes," Len replied. "And you know what the guy said? He said he didn't care about the tip at all—that it didn't matter one way or the other. He was just happy to have served the great Sandburg—that's what he said!"

Soon we arrived at the theatre for the first night of Norman Corwin's play entitled *The Rivalry,* an adaptation of the historic Lincoln-Douglas debates. Richard Boone starred as Lincoln, Martin Gabel portrayed Douglas, and Nancy Kelly was Mrs. Douglas. *The Rivalry* held more than passing interest for Carl, for his presence had been requested out front and backstage by his friend, Corwin, for whom Carl had deep affection.

After the show and the backstage amenities, the six of us gathered in front of the Bijou. Magically, a large Checker cab materialized before us. Two people got out; we six crammed in. Carl called out an address on East Sixty-second Street.

"Who lives there?" we asked eagerly.

"Tallulah Bankhead," Carl said. The name lingered magically in the crowded cab. "We've been invited."

As we approached the Bankhead brownstone, a curious sense of something missing swept over me. I felt lighthearted, even lightheaded—and lighthanded. Here I was on the way to a party with Carl Sandburg without our third body in tow. The guitar was missing! Tonight's party would be the first to which Carl ever invited me when a guitar was not only left behind but not even belatedly mentioned or missed at all.

We reached the front floor landing where Miss Bankhead was waiting. Tallulah Bankhead was not the tall, imperious image she projected on stage and screen. She was petite, a scant 5'3". When Carl Sandburg's head bent over in a kiss for the diminutive lady, it made an arc of white chalk against the wall of the dimly lit hall. Then the emotional Miss Bankhead gathered Carl into her arms in a wiry hug and kissed him repeatedly between husky baritone moans of "Da-ahling, da-ahling!"

We stepped from the gloom of the hall into the sitting room, cheerfully lit and comfortably furnished. I sensed that every item in it lived and breathed a story.

Carl introduced us each by name, with an affectionate biographical tagline by way of additional identification and his personal voucher for each one of us. For the moment, Miss Bankhead's effusiveness faded away, her theatrics subsided. Her large heavy-lidded eyes rested on us softly, calmly. She shook hands with each of us, with a clasp surprisingly firm for a hand so pale, delicate, and already blue-veined.

"I am very proud to meet Carl's friends," she said gravely.

In the script of the night ahead of us, I had only one line: a nervous, gulping "Howdayado." No one else, including Carl, had very much more to say, we began to realize as the night wore on. Carl Sandburg, not exactly known for his floor-yielding, met his match that night. Further, without his guitar, in whose partnership his voice could be heard in song at least, he was virtually silent, a strange, unreal Sandburg in a strange, unreal situation with one of the most fantastic, volatile, bombastic women of all time.

Despite the evidence before my eyes, the great actress never did seem real to me—certainly not the image of her I had brought with me—a collage of her public appearances and famous utterances, so undeviatingly identical with the Tallulah Bankhead in person that the fantasy was the fact. I was seeing her that night not from the vantage point of a comfortable chair in her living room, but as if I were on the edge of my seat in a movie theatre watching *Life Boat* or perched in a theatre balcony absorbing each word of *The Little Foxes*.

Soon after our arrival, Miss Bankhead's secretary appeared, a slender young man with reddish hair, a calm, quiet way of speaking, and beautiful manners. Although not markedly servile, he spoke only when spoken to. So unobtrusive, silent, and efficient was he that none of us could later recall his name beyond the hint that it began with a *T.* (Not until 1979–80 when the Backstage & Onstage Restaurants opened in New York's Broadway sector did "*T*"'s full name at last come to light: Ted Hook, the proprietor of the restaurants and a well-known figure in theatrical circles.) In contrast to his hyperactive boss, "*T*" was a small island of calm in the stormy Bankhead headquarters on Sixty-second street.

Miss Bankhead seldom spoke to young "T," but constantly gestured for drinks all around, mostly for her and for Carl. Bourbon was the order of the evening. "T" also had to double as Miss Bankhead's ever-ready cigarette producer and igniter and lipstick recoverer. Every twenty minutes or so, after having talked and eaten away the color glossing her mobile lips, Miss Bankhead would dab vigorously at her mouth with the lipstick and carelessly put it down. Then, moving compulsively from one part of the room to another, she would soon gesture for the lipstick again. Always at the ready, young "T" would recover the tube and plop it into her hand. Even as she was applying more vivid color to her lips, she talked and talked and smoked and smoked without a pause.

To and fro she rocked; back and forth she strode. She wore floppy, faded peach-colored lounging pajamas, styled in the thirties of heavy silk, but she wore them with great panache and class. The generous bell-bottoms flapped audibly about her elegant legs when she swiftly changed course in her turns about the room.

She stopped from time to time in a clearing before the fireplace. Above her, covering the whole area of wall between fireplace mantle and ceiling, hung a painting which bore the unmistakable stamp of a style of the late twenties. A charming, arresting example it was, too, a quasi-life-sized portrait of an elegant young girl with fine-boned patrician features—Tallulah Bankhead in her mid-twenties. She is seated, thoughtful, almost wistful, and very composed, wearing a filmy gown of pastel pink and plum dappled with impressionistic paler colors. The painter was an avant-garde artist, Augustus John. To be painted by the celebrated bohemian in those post-World War I days in London was to attain sure and solid celebrity, like the famous subjects of John Singer Sargent of an earlier time and Salvador Dali of this era. (Picasso once described John as "the best bad painter in England.") When suddenly juxtaposed with the whirling, oscillating figure of Miss Bankhead, the freely, boldly painted portrait became static, like a figure in an Egyptian frieze.

Miss Bankhead would pause for an instant before her portrait, as if she were an extension of it. She would then resume her circumnavigation of the room, bourbon-baritoned words falling tumultuously from rouge-smeared lips. Her clouds of cigarette smoke obscured the portrait, then slowly cleared. She waved her hands in emphasis of some point, in one hand a drink, in the other, the ever-present cigarette, her sixth finger.

The famous portrait now hangs in the National Portrait Gallery in Washington, D.C., where Miss Bankhead's father, Speaker of the House William B., and her uncle, Alabama Senator John H., made their marks in Congress more than a generation before.

Those of us who that night comprised Miss Bankhead's audience were barely settled with our drinks when our hostess apologized for the lack of food. "There simply isn't a thing in the house to eat, is there, da-ahling?" she said to her secretary, who nodded solemn confirmation.

We attached no particular significance to that announcement early in the evening when hunger had yet to grip us, thanks to our bountiful Sardi's meal. As for Miss Bankhead, I mused, her steady intake of lipstick would sustain her.

And bourbon. On the far side of the room adjoining the room where we sat, I could see a formidable array of amber bottles glowing in the half-light on the sideboard. The cupboard may have been bare at the Bankhead bailiwick that night, but the bourbon abounded. Hour passed hour. With mechanical frequency, Miss Bankhead's arm shot out like a railroad signal. Into the hand "T" plopped another bourbon and water, interspersed with an occasional cigarette or lipstick. Almost as often, Carl was served a straight one. As bourbon followed bourbon, Sandburg's famous iron stomach, growing emptier of food, began to rumble rebelliously, almost in tune with mine.

Miss Bankhead was telling us with a certain pride of a respiratory disorder she had contracted.

"Hyperventilation," she drawled proudly. "Sometimes when you take a deep breath, you pass out." She added dramatically that only high-strung, creative types were likely to be visited by this chic condition.

A peek at my watch revealed that it was 2:30 A.M. Miss Bankhead was off on a new monologue, her favorite subject: the men in her family, now long dead. Her voice changed from hoarse histrionics to hushed reverence.

Although Carl had early given up any idea of equal talking time with Miss Bankhead, he managed to wedge in at this juncture a word or two of his admiration for Miss Bankhead's father. As Southern legislators went, Carl ventured to say, William Bankhead as Speaker of the House from 1936 to 1940 had shown a liberalism unusual for a son of the Solid South, whose political climate was one of doctrinaire reaction to Roosevelt's "radical" measures. Moreover, Carl noted, bringing in his favorite numerological game, William Bankhead was the more distinguished for having lived to the age of sixty-six, a number divisible by eleven.

If Carl had not previously wrapped up Miss Bankhead's heart and put it in his pocket, he had surely done so now. She embraced him worshipfully and kissed his flushed cheeks.

Carl had had his say. After that I cannot remember if he uttered even one word. Miss Bankhead, her father's daughter, took up the gavel and resumed her role as speaker of her house. Soon she introduced her next great hero, His Holiness Pope John XXIII. While her reverence for him did not fully match what she felt for her father or Carl Sandburg, her admiration for him was considerable, especially considering that she was not of his faith.

She told of having seen the pope that evening on television in the high and solemn ceremony of admitting into the priesthood seminarians who had journeyed to the Vatican from all parts of the world. She described how John, the highest member of the Catholic Church, indeed the Vicar of Christ himself, had knelt and humbly kissed the feet of these lowliest of rank in the echelons of the Church. A true actress, proud of her craft, she was in turn proud of this new pope, this great trouper who headed a cast of millions. Miss Bankhead paused in her eulogy. She looked down at Carl Sandburg's feet. Our eyes followed hers.

Carl was shoeless.

At some point in the long evening Carl had decided to remove his shoes. As might be expected, his feet had begun to ache and swell a bit. Now as I looked at Carl's feet, I saw a startling departure from the otherwise dark "evening clothes" effect of his attire: he was wearing brown socks. They were woolen, heavy in weight, rough-knit, and wrinkled.

Miss Bankhead for once was speechless. She gazed at Carl's brown-socked feet. As if on cue, she fell to her knees before Carl and tenderly took one of his feet in her hands. Looking up worshipfully, tossing back her blondish mane, she declared defiantly, "If Pope John can kiss the feet of the new priests, I guess I can kiss the feet of Carl Sandburg."

She easily removed the garterless socks. They reached up slightly into the territory of Carl's gray long johns. Carl's feet were white and elegant and free of any blemish.

Miss Bankhead bent over and kissed the feet of her beloved Carl Sandburg.

Then she gently pulled Carl's socks back on, even remembering to secure the tops under the ends of the long johns. She found his shoes, slipped them on his feet, laced them, and set his feet back on the floor.

During this entire ceremony, Carl could only chuckle and utter a demurring "Aw, shucks."

Climactic as this scene was, it was far from the third act curtain. We had ahead of us several more hours of drinking, following Miss Bankhead's dramatic movements, and listening to the boom of her baritone voice as she flitted from one fascinating subject to another with scarcely a pause.

Several more foodless hours lay ahead of us. What had begun to disturb me now was another kind of vitamin deficiency—the absence of Vitamin G as in guitar.

To us guitar people, food and liquor could be eschewed, but the guitar was essential. What was a party without one? How could other people claim to have had any fun at a party without a guitar kicking around as a common denominator—especially if Carl Sandburg was guest of honor? Long before other parties had reached this present stage, somebody, somewhere in the house would be playing a guitar. Of course, there was always singing, and there Carl always shone. Carl needed music more than he needed food—or even bourbon.

But here at Miss Bankhead's there were no songs to counter the drinking; it was an even more serious lack than food. All we had between drinks was drinks—each one falling ominously into emptier and emptier stomachs, with no music in the air to dissipate the fumes of the alcohol.

As the first streaks of dawn began to shoot across the eastern sky, I realized with alarm that this new day was a working day. Fortunately, none of us was required to punch an early-morning clock. Nevertheless, the rosy fingers of the new dawn seemed to point to the exit.

For the last half-hour, Carl had not only sat silent and motionless, he seemed actually graven in his chair. Even his drinking arm had ceased its up and down movement. His face was fixed in a ruddy half-smile, but his eyes were glassy.

We all rose to our feet and went for our things in the other room. When we returned, Carl still sat in his chair. He had not stirred. His only movement had been to sink even deeper into the chair. He made an effort to rise, but fell back again.

There was no question about it. Carl was crocked. Undistracted for hours by eating, music, and conversation that permitted dialogue, he had overshot the finish line of his set drinking limit, but silently, sweetly, and in great dignity, giving trouble to nobody.

We said our good nights. It was kissing time again—facial, not pedal—and I got in line to receive my farewell Bankhead buss and to hear myself called "Da-ahling." For a few hours of my life I had been deliriously swept up in a Bankhead whirlwind. For the first time for as far back as I could remember, I had gotten through a guitar-less party without once wishing to flee the boredom. I would no more have wanted to leave Miss Bankhead's that night than I would have left her performance in *The Little Foxes* before the final curtain.

Brawny Len Steckler got Carl down the stairs and into a taxi with Virginia and Olga. They headed for Virginia's flat on East Twenty-seventh Street. Since noise and blasting on the construction site across from Henderson Place had preempted Carl's visit to his usual New York headquarters, he was settled comfortably into Virginia's walkup flat for this visit.

Much later that morning, I awoke to the tattoo of a bourbonic hammer at my temples. My first thought was of Carl and of how he had weathered the rigors of the bibulous evening. I phoned Virginia's flat. Carl himself answered.

He sounded bright and cheerful, boomy and hearty—as if *he* had no trace of headache or shake.

"I guess I did have a bit too much last night," he said. He paused for a moment. "It's the first time in my life I ever hung up my pants without first emptying the pockets!"

Steichen
the Photographer

SOMETIME IN 1960, Carl Sandburg sent a short note to Harry Golden, who was then putting together a biography-memoir of Carl, hitting highlights of the poet's life from birth, in 1878, to 1961. The note was a request—nay, an order—that Golden include in his book the names of the three persons who had exerted the greatest influence in Sandburg's life.

The first of these, Carl wrote, was Phillip Green Wright, his teacher at Lombard College in Galesburg, Illinois. Wright was political and literary mentor for the young student Sandburg. The other two influences Carl found in the family—his wife Paula and her brother, Edward Steichen.

When Sandburg married Lilian "Paula" Steichen on June 15, 1908, brother Ed did not lose a sister, he gained a brother, and a big brother at that. Carl was all of fourteen months his senior. From the beginning, the two brothers-in-law hit it off. Though related only by marriage they became even closer than blood brothers and lived for sixty years always keenly in touch with each other. Indeed, across those years, there developed between the two the warmest, most moving in-law relationship since Ruth and Naomi of the Bible.

While most men draw an insurance adjuster, an accountant, or a dress manufacturer for a brother-in-law, Carl Sandburg drew a genius. Edward Steichen was indeed a latter-day Leonardo da Vinci as Sandburg fondly labeled him: mechanic, plant breeder, geneticist, painter, scientist, mathematician, and photographer.

Photography was always Steichen's chief obsession. He nurtured and indulged it more than he did his other talents, and gave to the world some of the greatest works of portrait art that ever found their way through camera lens onto photographic plate, finally to endure for all time on paper.

Sandburg, the family scrivener, couldn't wait to commit to manuscript the story of his brother-in-law's great wisdom and accomplishments. He fervently felt that Ed was an embodiment of the great ideal, "toils, hardships, and dangers (being) little or nothing to him alongside of the American Dream." So he wrote to Harry Golden in 1960.

Sandburg's literary output by 1929 was prodigious: five volumes of poetry, the two volumes of *Abraham Lincoln: The Prairie Years, Rootabaga Stories* for children, and *The American Songbag*. At twenty-six, he had been eager to write about Norse heroes—in ancestral pride, perhaps—but never got to it. His excursions into the Lincoln biography demanded painstaking research. Now, at fifty-one, with a live hero easy to reach, to interview, but more happily, a member of his own family, he could write a special biography, a portrait, a salute to his brother-in-law Edward Steichen. Its title, *Steichen the Photographer,* was to the point, clear to the eye, easy to read, and easy to say. But Carl, incorrigible juggler of words and conjurer of tongue twisters, loved to challenge people to say "biographer of a photographer" with the ease that he could say it, adding "If you can say it distinctly, then you're definitely sober."

Steichen the Photographer was probably the easiest book Sandburg had written up to that time and following, because love was the principal component. He could express love more felicitously and effortlessly than any other writer in English. The language of love flowed from him like a freshet. Never platitudinous or mushy or maudlin, its supply was inexhaustible, fed as it was by the deep, ever-renewing spring of his simple sincerity.

Carl's fond and frankly loving memoir of Steichen was too little, too soon; as year upon year passed, and the famed photographer piled achievement upon achievement, this became more and more evident. Carl was not unaware of the incompleteness of his biography; he acknowledged this in his foreword to the book. Besides, its first and only edition (later, sixty percent of it became part of *The Sandburg Range,* Harcourt Brace, 1957) was limited to 925 copies. In 1929 Steichen was only fifty years old. Carl said it all succinctly in this simple phrase: "On the day that God made Ed, He didn't do anything else but sit around and feel good."

The crowning achievement of Steichen's career came during his tenure as director of the Department of Photography of the Museum of Modern Art. In 1955 he conceived and assembled a mighty show of photographs, all of them the work of dedicated camera magicians the world over, showing humankind being born, living, loving, laughing, praying, and dying. The exhibit, 503 pieces from sixty-eight countries, opened at the museum on January 24, 1955; *The Family of Man* was its title.

Shortly after the opening of the exhibit, the museum published a volume of the inspired Steichen selections. It is a beautiful book, with a beautiful prologue. For this section, Steichen sought someone who could write with sensitivity, who loved humanity, and who had a bit of the poet in him. There was Carl, already sharpening his pencils and adjusting his green visor in anticipation of the job that was not only up his alley, but would also make him a kind of partner in this historical milestone of documentary photography. Pictures by Edward Steichen; words by Carl Sandburg—brother-in-law.

The 503 pieces which made up what was the greatest exhibition of photography ever assembled, introduced by the Sandburg prologue, were bound together between the hard covers of a durable book. In the summer of 1959, after a tour of the United States and the Western world, *The Family of Man* got a bid from the East: Russia, anxious to see the exhibit, indicated she would lift the Iron Curtain for a peek at it. Under State Department auspices, then, the package was set for a Moscow opening in July. Along with it, and to show they were for real, went the two octogenarian brothers-in-law from the Occident, Ed Steichen and Carl Sandburg.

The year 1959 was one of the busiest in Sandburg's life. He dedicated three high schools and one elementary school named for him; went to Stockholm for Swedish American Day to receive an award from King Gustav; on Lincoln's birthday, addressed a joint session of Congress, members of the Supreme Court, the Cabinet, and diplomatic corps; and went to Moscow with Steichen to open *The Family of Man*. The high point of those activities, in point of national historical significance, would probably have to be the Lincoln Day address, at which he neither sang nor played guitar.

But the Moscow junket started out as more fun. On July 19, 1959, the eve of their departure, The Silly Center Opera Company and its privileged coterie of "subscribers" assembled at Henderson Place and threw a big noisy bon voyage party for the two bold venturers into the inscrutable East. No ceremonious address by Carl was called for, beyond addressing himself to song, guitar, food, fun, and bourbon, amidst a joint session of his New York friends: his scrivening colleagues and his fellow members of The Society of the Classic Guitar.

Frugal, canny Carl had other work to do on the eve of the Russian trip. He gave his attention to an offer of a series of radio commercials for American Airlines, readings of his own writings, strictly dignified, of an institutional nature. Carl arrived in New York a week before his scheduled departure to Moscow so that he would be under no pressure for time during the negotiations.

This freedom from pressure, besides resulting in a fair deal, brought him an even fairer bonus. In charge of his jaunts hither and yon about New York was the fair young Joanna Taub of Young and Rubicam, the advertising agency handling the American Airlines account.

But on the day of the party, it was Carl who did the squiring; he took charge of Joanna and brought her along, little knowing just how fatefully he was in charge of her. Carl proudly presented Joanna to everybody—to his guitar friends and colleagues—and also, of course, to his co-guest of honor, brother-in-law Edward Steichen. Steichen was a widower then. I remember him on that day clearly. He was charming and hearty, tall and straight, jolly and animated—his eye as keen for a pretty girl as was his brother's-in-law.

Steichen's left arm was in a sling that day, but it did not affect his other movements nor did he ever evince pain. Rather, it gave him a swashbuckling, picaresque air. He had hurt his arm in an accident.

"Skating," he explained. Skating at eighty!

The party went on into the night. Carl and Edward left a day later for Moscow to carry on their work for *The Family of Man,* doing what they could to hasten the thawing of the Cold War by the warmth of their own simple, open personalities and the human camera testament they took with them.

Shortly after the brothers-in-law returned from Moscow, Steichen was felled by a stroke. Joanna Taub, capable and patient, was near him always, nursing him through the dark days of the siege. As recovery came slowly but surely, she received and accepted Steichen's proposal of marriage. They were married June 5, 1960.

To journalist and old family friend Joe Wershba, Paula Sandburg said firmly, unequivocally: "My brother owes his life to that girl."

Often have the walls of Henderson Place rung loud with the sounds of music, laughter, and lighthearted fun. But some parties can have a more serious ending—like marriage, for instance.

Sandburg didn't write the biography of his photographer brother-in-law until twenty-one years after they officially became relatives. But Steichen didn't wait to ply his art. He fell to the task immediately, even before his sister became Carl's wife, and began probing the poet's rugged features with his faithful third eye—the camera lens. During his distinguished career, culminating in the colossal *Family of Man* collection, Edward Steichen held on to his title as official photographer of the family of one man: Carl Sandburg. Faithfully, he posed and photographed Carl and Paula, then the children, then the grandchildren, when they came. His work—especially the family shots—is never pretentious. Steichen went about his duties with the simple directness and diligence of any earnest, dedicated local photographer of weddings, babies, graduations, and communions.

In 1939, *Abraham Lincoln: The War Years* was published, Carl Sandburg's greatest work if a Pulitzer Prize carries any weight. At the peak of his creative life, Carl was also in peak condition. The physical beauty of his face in Steichen's photo of him that year truly represents Carl Sandburg at sixty-one. Steichen's camera never lied, euphemized, or idolized. Rather, it brought out extra dimensions, made new discoveries, offered keener insights of his subjects. I believe Steichen's photograph of Carl Sandburg at sixty-one is the greatest he ever made. I will say it, the ghosts of Shaw, Duse, Rodin, Valentino, Greta Garbo, and J. P. Morgan notwithstanding, and let them haunt me forever if they like.

Book and portrait appeared simultaneously. Carl's *Lincoln* was a monument of writing; Steichen's Sandburg, a monument of photography—a work which Carl describes in a letter to his brother-in-law as a "processional montage of six shifting phizzogs."

The six phizzogs are in profile, disembodied heads against a black background; they move kinetically to the right in irregular procession. An unearthly light—its source could be Steichen's private patch of blue heaven—falls gently upon and around the soft contours of Sandburg's features. Routine photogeneity is transcended here. The photograph becomes Sandburg's memorial image for all time.

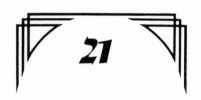

Smoke in Your Eyes

ON MARCH 22, 1958, I AWOKE at my usual hour of ten A.M. What was my program for that day? I switched on the knob of my memory, saw the picture, groaned, and switched it off again.

The picture I saw was the boiler room in our basement, and flashing across the screen insistently, like an emergency signal, were the urgent words: "To be cleaned! Today! Today!"

I had chosen that day because, as far as I knew, it was free and clear of any commitments. Carl Sandburg, up in his room, and soon to descend for our usual leisurely and wordy breakfast, had said a session with Caedmon Records would keep him out for the whole day. Carl had barely finished his second cup of coffee when our bell rang, and there at the door was an eager emissary from Caedmon to whisk him away to the recording studios.

Now I could tackle the boiler room. It was in such a state of chaos and neglect that it actually posed a grave danger. A good part of the rubble was an accumulation of residue house paints, too long forgotten—and half-empty, ill-corked bottles of paint remover, benzine, shellacs, and other volatile agents whose fumes, exposed to even a hint of a spark, could blow us all out of this life.

With Sandburg in the house, and everyday at breakfast in the kitchen uncomfortably adjacent to the boiler room, my apprehension over this potential time bomb began to mount with each passing hour.

If Carl was to attain his next goal of reaching an age divisible by eleven—he'd made his previous one three years before at seventy-seven—I decided he'd better stop having breakfast next to the boiler room, or even quit Henderson Place altogether.

Or I could simply go into the arsenal and defuse the bombs.

Five hours later, grimy, grubby, and growling, I emerged from my labors. The nail of my *anular* (ring) finger had been broken to the quick; my hands were numb, swollen, and pulsating; my back was thrown out, and my nose and throat lined with soot. It was nearly six o'clock. I called to Terry, wherever she might be in the house; there was no answer. First, I would have a leisurely bath; after that, a rest for an hour or so; then dinner in the kitchen with Sandburg—a safe and relaxed meal, this time. All of these calming effects might even help steady my hand for my fine-lined brush drawing later.

The doorbell rang sharply three times when I was halfway up the stairs. Wearily, I stomped down. It was Terry, smiling and rosy-cheeked from the March wind on her face. She was laden with bundles.

"You'll never guess what happened when you were in the cata-combs! I didn't want to disturb you, so . . ."

"Never mind that," I said testily. "What are all those bundles about?"

"Dinner!" she answered. "I've been out for hours! First I had to go clear down to the Spanish section of Fourteenth Street for saffron, then to the Fulton Fish Market for shrimps and clams, then I had to go back for chickens . . ."

"Sounds like a plot for a paella," I said. "What are we doing with paella tonight, anyway? Didn't you say that you had an old stew in the freezer?"

"Not with Segovia coming and Olga Coelho, Ethel Smith, Len and Olga, Dolores, Irwin—the whole gang, in fact . . . PLUS . . ."

The weight of my just-completed labors was suddenly more than I could crawl out from under. "Plus who?" I asked weakly.

"Mimsi, Leonard, and Robin . . . and Robin is bringing his folks," Terry added brightly. I knew who Robin's folks were.

They were Ella and Otto Harbach.

Otto Harbach! I was immediately revitalized. Only a few weeks before, I had found myself giving fervent blessing upon oft-maligned television when I realized that it was bringing to me one of the most heart-rending moments I had ever experienced in years of watching that illuminated rectangle. I had turned on the set without purpose or plan, and I saw that a musical program was in progress. Soon it became clear that homage was being paid Otto Harbach. A little while later, Harbach was chanting his own lyrics for "Smoke Gets in Your Eyes." The patrician gentleman, his face like an ancient, handsome ruin, was then well into his eighties, and now he was saying the romantic lines of the beautiful song in a husky, tremulous voice with profound emotion and nuance. Over the years of his long life, he had not forgotten the art of spellbindery, which had won for him and his school, Knox College, first prize in the Interstate Intercollegiate oratorical contest in 1895. All of Galesburg, Illinois, home of Knox College and birthplace of Carl Sandburg, rejoiced that night, Sandburg among the most vociferous. Harbach, then twenty-three, five years older than Carl, was a campus hero, and all night, a mob of hundreds of celebrants gathered on the college grounds cheering, yelling, singing, and dancing around bonfires.

As I watched Harbach on the television screen, I could well understand how people could idolize this elegant and poetic hero of another era. Yes, smoke swirled around me and got into my eyes—and tears welled up . . . and in a few hours, he would be in my house.

And Segovia, and Coelho, and Smith—et al—and of course Sandburg, who was already there, the rallying figure whose presence brought a legion of friends from all walks of life.

Now Terry was adding her bundles to those already piled up on the kitchen table. I caught a whiff of the sea still lingering among the shrimps and the clams; and Spain itself was evoked through the pungent aroma of the saffron.

It all happened in a flash. While I was hermetically sealed in the boiler room, Terry explained to me, a phone call came from Mimsi, our next-door neighbor in Number 10. She was expecting her friend Robin Harbach that evening with his father and mother and hoped that she could bring them over to see Sandburg.

The chain that went from Mimsi to Otto Harbach began when Mimsi was married to a writer who was a friend of the Harbachs. After divorcing him, Mimsi married her doctor. A few years later, she divorced *him* and immediately became a Harbach herself; she married Robin, her third husband.

Sixty-four years before, when Carl Sandburg saw Otto Harbach in his glory on the Knox College campus, he was a wide-eyed kid of fifteen, still on a milk route. He had four years yet to go before he, too, would be enrolled in college. Carl did not attend Knox, but Lombard College, close by in Galesburg. Lombard College was later taken over by Knox. Thus, Knox was understandably close to Carl, almost his own alma mater, making him all the more proud of its illustrious alumnus, Otto Harbach.

But on that June night in 1895, Carl could not get near the mobbed Harbach. He could only worship his hero from afar. He did not actually meet him until 1939, in New York.

As these years passed, curiously, the paths of Carl Sandburg and Otto Harbach never crossed. Both had been very much aware of each other's existence, following with keen interest and pride the triumphs and the successes that came in their chosen fields, one a writer of musical plays and lyrics, the other, a writer of history, biography, and poetry, both troubadours and incurable romantics. Both were well along in years when they first met in 1939, although in spirit they had really been friends for decades.

There was lots of talking to be done, and after they met, Carl visited the Harbachs regularly when business or pleasure took him to New York.

They visited often during the forties and early fifties. Then the visits diminished and soon after, ceased altogether. Harbach's health had begun to fail.

This night at Henderson Place would be the first time the two had been together for several years.

Following a long hiatus, Segovia and Sandburg were also to be reunited that night. In a few hours, all were to gather at Henderson Place.

Despite my broken fingernail, sooty throat and nostrils, shaky hands, aching muscles, and out-of-whack-roliliac, I was exceedingly happy over the prospect of the evening before us. I rejoiced in my good fortune to have a wife in the house who could take command and carry on the social and cultural activities under its roof, while I was incommunicado in the gaseous boiler room down below, attending to the prosaic matter of keeping that roof from blowing off.

I had met that deadline. What about the other—ominous in its own way—my cartoon deadline that I'd planned to start working on after dinner? What about it indeed? I bristled resentfully, mutinous at the thought. My syndicate didn't know it, I decided grimly, but its gaping maw, into which I had fed more than 5,000 drawings with clocklike regularity for over eighteen years, would have to go hungry for a day or so, and hang the consequences. I was proud of that record I'd posted, but I was not in the least disturbed; I was even glad to be missing my first deadline. I felt a curious elation: much as I loved my artwork and was proud to be of that profession, I felt no disloyalty in deserting it tonight for the fascinating world that the guitar had made for me.

I would now give the party my full attention. I saw immediately that it was to be one of our most exciting parties at Henderson Place. Spontaneous parties are bound to be the most fun. The spontaneity was reflected in the gaiety and ebullience of the guests. Almost on a moment's notice, I marveled, we had been able to assemble a score of friends from all parts of the city, in many walks of life, of varying degrees of age, from different ethnic and religious backgrounds, all of them drawn by the same magnet—Carl Sandburg.

As a cook in the Spanish tradition, Terry surpassed herself that night. Her paella was even worthy of an Andalusian—one who was worldly wise, well traveled, and a hypercritical gourmet, especially of his native cuisine. There was such an Andalusian among our guests— Andrés Segovia—and he had three helpings of the paella, blessing Terry with each one.

The Silly Center Opera Company had a small and lively revival that night. Most of its cast was present: Irwin Hasen, Dolores Wilson, Len and Olga Steckler, and Eric Ericson. Olga Coelho sang, Carl sang. Segovia played even on my unworthy guitar. How could he have refused that night on any count? Three of Sandburg's favorite ladies, Virginia Pasley, Catherine McCarthy, and her sister Anne, were among the audience, and during the evening the audience grew and grew as new arrivals appeared—some invited, some not. The grapevine was indeed humming that night.

I wish I could say that the pièce de résistance of the evening was a recitation of "Smoke Gets In Your Eyes" by Harbach. Yes, even after Segovia's playing, Sandburg's and Coelho's singing, the performance of *La Traviata* by The Silly Center Opera Company, Terry's paella, my harrowing story of my toil in the boiler room—what a dramatic climax to a memorable evening it would have made, if Harbach had only consented to do it. But he could not. One could see that he was too old and enfeebled to do anything but chat with Sandburg and listen to the music and fun, and even that seemed an effort. Now I was all the more grateful for having seen Harbach that one fortuitous moment on television.

Carl and Harbach sat together and recapitulated their lives during the last few years when their visits had broken off. During all this, I was studying Carl's demeanor; every minute he sat with Harbach, he was respectful, attentive, deferential. I had never seen him in such awe—even with so great a personage as Segovia in the same room.

But to understand, I had merely to go back with Carl to that June night in 1895, on the Knox College campus and see again an ungainly, pigeon-toed boy barely in his teens, gaze proudly and lovingly upon Galesburg's great hero—sophisticated Otto Harbach who'd brought such honor to his school and to Carl's home town.

And tonight Carl was gazing upon his hero no less fervently. But there was also another factor behind Carl's reverential behavior toward Harbach that night.

He had respect for his elders.

With sudden impact, I realized that never before had I seen Sandburg in the company of anyone older than he. Harbach was a mature eighty-seven then; Sandburg, a gangling, adolescent eighty-two.

The time came for Harbach and his company to go. The two old men embraced each other fondly, recalling again the phenomenon of their separation for forty-four years.

They said their goodbyes.

It was the last time they saw each other. Harbach died in 1963.

They had met for the first time amid music, laughter, and gaiety, and parted the same way almost twenty years later.

The Everloving, Everkind, Undersigned

THE BOOKS WHICH CARL SANDBURG left behind him, warmly inscribed after visits, were the *present juste* to his hosts and hostesses, next to the pleasant memory of his company. When he ran out of his own books, he was sure to have extra copies of other writers' books around that would do almost as well. The point was, he made any book extra special when it included a personal inscription by his own hand.

Sandburg's salutations were always super-salutary and heartfelt; they set you up for the day. They had you hugging yourself. They restored a flagging self-confidence. Maudlin over-reaction? As a recipient of such Sandburg largesse, I checked my feelings with those of others I knew. Mine were conservative by comparison.

A favorite Sandburg accolade, laid carefully and discriminatingly only on the deserving, was "You ain't what's wrong with the world." When he said it, or wrote it, the tacit rejoinder, "or right with the world," never occurred to you, because you knew that cynicism was not in Carl's makeup. He truly trusted you with the world, the same one he lived in, the same one William O. Douglas lived in. In 1958

$\mathcal{E}$dward Steichen and Olga Steckler (wife of Len, behind the camera) at Henderson Place, July 19, 1959. Sketches on the wall above them are of the Missus, Terry, drawn by yours truly.

$\mathcal{S}$andburg, Ethel Smith, and Steichen joined in festive song the night before the two gents left for Russia, July 19, 1959. (Photo by Len Steckler.)

$\mathcal{E}$thel Smith was a diminutive dynamo in our fun-loving guitar coterie. Best known standing at the organ for her rendition of that brilliant Brazilian samba, "Tico, Tico" (in the film "Bathing Beauties", with Esther Williams and Red Skelton), Ethel also fascinated Carl with her comedy songs and skillful guitar accompaniments. Len Steckler took this picture at my Tudor City digs in 1950.

*M*arilyn laughing and Carl amused, captured in a moment of humor at Len Steckler's studio. Len took both of these pictures in December, 1961, nine short months before Marilyn Monroe's tragic death on August 5, 1962.

*C*arl and Marilyn Monroe became friends when he was in Hollywood, working with filmmaker George Stevens on the screenplay of "The Greatest Story Ever Told". Carl was always partial to having beautiful women near him, though his deportment was never anything other than gentlemanly. Carl often enlisted his women companions in taking dictation, as when a poem or flash of inspiration would seize him. Marilyn Monroe sometimes found herself in this "secretarial" role, and it delighted her.

*T*erry's Camp Fire girls told the life story of Abraham Lincoln in Indian symbols; Michael Caputo took this picture at Henderson Place, March 1958.

*A*nother Indian scroll translation; this one is of an untitled poem from Carl's *The People, Yes.* Carl was ever respectful in blue-serge. On the right is the Missus, Terry; next to her is Stephanie Lange. The picture was snapped by June Havoc, Gypsy Rose Lee's sister. The scroll is on view in the museum at Connemara Farm, the Sandburg home, in Flat Rock, North Carolina.

*C*arl was an unforgettable study. I drew him in quick gesture style many times from life. Later, this image became so deeply engraved on my vision that I could draw him from memory with ease—writing, smoking, playing the guitar, or carrying his beloved instrument in its case.

eeing this sketch of mine, Carl sighed a deep "Hmmm," then pushed the visor away from his eyes. He said wryly, "ain't exactly an Arrow Collar ad, am I?"

alking near Henderson Place, in Carl Schurz Park, on Manhattan's Upper East Side, I was struck by the matching profiles of Carl Sandburg and John Huston Finley, editor of the New York Times 1920-1930. Sandburg's cheroot made a visual distinction between them. Carl was fascinated by Finley's walks around the perimeter of Manhattan Island, an exercise undertaken annually by Finley, and written up for the great daily's readers.

I made this drawing of Carl while he was booming out a song on April 3, 1957.

Sandburg wrote the colorful Supreme Court justice: "You ain't what's wrong with this country."

I never saw Sandburg hold pen in mid-air over the flyleaf of a book, saying, "Let me see—what shall I write?" He had a reservoir of words and phrases all his own. They belonged to him as if he were their inventor. Words like "fellowship," "brotherhood," and "fraternal" were used at their 100 percent unadulterated meanings. The passing years of creeping cynicism and ever-widening social gaps rampant in the world could never devalue these words when Carl used them. Close friends, members of his family, and particularly children rated a booming "I love you a million bushels"; phrases more romantic and poetic such as "lucky stars be yours," and "the peace of great phantoms be for you" often flowed gracefully from his stubby pen. Carl dashed off "scrivener," "loving heart"—and "irrefragable" without a speck of hesitation. On sight, these inscriptions instantly conjured up his presence. You said, "Carl Sandburg was here."

Not all of the inscriptions which follow were addressed to individuals within the circle of Sandburg's New York guitar friends. We of the guitar coterie concede that there *is* another life apart from the guitar, and that man *can* live without it, as did other New Yorkers, old friends of Carl's who became friends of mine, and who wander in and out of the pages of this book at various times.

I had known Sandburg barely two weeks when I made his book-gift list. In the fall of 1948, he dropped off *Remembrance Rock* and in it wrote his inscription. Its personal touch was there in its reference to a kindred interest, the guitar:

> *For Gregory d'Alessio*
> *as a beginner*
> *to an adept*
> *with salutations*
>
> *Carl Sandburg*
> *1   9   4   8*

Other books, other inscriptions came along regularly, but the high point came in 1957 with the gift of Sandburg's six-volume *Lincoln.* My wife had soon become part of every salutation, kindness, and thoughtfulness that Carl showed toward me, and now we shared billing in his inscriptions. In fact, the Missus got top billing in the Lincoln inscription:

For Terry and Greg
from the fourth floor grenadier
Honorary Member of the S.C.G.
graduate hobo,
poet-in-ordinary
so-so singer
bemedalled & bifurcated

Carl Sandburg
1   9   5   7

The reference to his bemedallment was the honor conferred upon him five years before by the National Institute and American Academy of Arts. His bifurcation was just an alliterative funny, he said; at first he'd thought of writing "bewitched, bothered, and bemedalled," but on second thought he felt that it would sound too much like the song from *Pal Joey*.

C. D. Batchelor, Batch, as Carl Sandburg and every other good friend called the *New York News* Pulitzer Prize–winning cartoonist, first met Carl when they were fellow newspapermen and admirers of Joseph Medill Patterson, publisher and founder of the *New York News* and the *Chicago Tribune*. Batch's apartment in New York was the modestly furnished penthouse mentioned earlier in this memoir. Batch's penthouse was extolled in an inscription in *The Prairie Years*. Sandburg wrote:

For C. D. Batchelor who is hopelessly Midwest as most of the folks in this
book and who has been a witness of squatter sovereignty in a Manhattan
Penthouse

Carl Sandburg
June   1 9 4 3

In *Remembrance Rock*, just after Batchelor's marriage, Sandburg wrote:

For C. D. and Julie Batchelor—instead of rice and old shoes and in lieu of
flowers and flagons and remembering a pleasant work corner loaned to the
scrivener here of

The Ever-loving, Ever-kind, Undersigned

Carl Sandburg
1 9 4 8

Sandburg gave the Batchelors a copy of his friend Louis Untermeyer's *Modern American Poetry,* inscribing it:

Dear Batch and Julie

Since you live in a poem of a house
why not have these 438 poems around?
Says the Old Inhabitant

Carl
1950

In his own *Complete Poems* Carl wrote:

For C. D. and Julie Batchelor in whose domicile and environs some of these ectoplastic creations came into light and being for which praise the Lord who is Almighty and may help us in this time of storm

Carl Sandburg
Anno Domini
1 9 5 0

Carl Sandburg's vintage friendship with Hazel Buchbinder was telling in its high points of memories, poignant, gay, serious—and one, at first dark and menacing, which turned to light. A noted composer-arranger, Mrs. Buchbinder helped Sandburg through the onerous task he took upon himself in gathering the 280 songs which made up *The American Songbag.* When the book finally appeared, Carl wrote into it for his fellow toiler:

This book for
Hazel Felman Buchbinder
friend and co-laborer
in this zigzag adventure
and tumultuous enterprise

Carl Sandburg
Chicago 1927

Then, almost a quarter of a century later, Hazel received another book of songs from Sandburg. This was *The New American Songbag,* a

151

collection of fifty-nine songs, twenty of which were encores from the first *Songbag*. Three of these twenty were Hazel's own fine arrangements of "Old Abe Lincoln Came Out of the Wilderness," "I Don't Like No Railroad Man," and the perennial "Wanderin'," mainstay in the repertoire of every baritone and basso worthy of the name "robust." Carl wrote:

> *For Hazel Buchbinder*
> *With whom I have*
> *laughter and tears*
> *—ever with prayers*
> *and deep good wishes*
> *Carl Sandburg*
> *1   9   5   1*

Hazel and Dr. Jacob Buchbinder's home in Chicago was the gathering place for writers, artists, and musicians in the days of Sandburg's newspaper work in that city. It was at the Buchbinders' in 1938 where he first met his great idol of the guitar, Andrés Segovia, and where he fell in love with a gramophone voice and a song: Olga Coelho singing "Meu Limon, Meu Limeiro."

With Hazel one of the collaborators on the *Songbag,* Jake became Sandburg's favorite punster-playmate and doctor. In 1941, when Sandburg's daughter Helga developed complications in the course of the birth of her first child, John Carl, it was Dr. Buchbinder who saved the lives of both baby and mother with his surgeon's skill. Sandburg fervently acknowledged that gift.

One of the shortest inscriptions Carl ever wrote summed up most poignantly this long friendship with the Buchbinders:

> *Hazel*
> *with so many great,*
> *gay and dark memories*
> *Carl*

When Sandburg wanted to find a guitar teacher for his grandosn John Carl, he turned to his friend Segovia for advice. Segovia recommended Sophocles Papas, distinguished guitarist and teacher whose school for the guitar was located in Washington, D.C.

Carl and Sophocles became fast friends, and Carl's appreciation for his teacher-friend never waned.

Maestro Segovia's endorsement was translated into poetic terms by Sandburg in an inscription in *The Sandburg Range:*

> *Sophocles Papas*
>
> *a great apostle, great teacher*
> *of the guitar*
> *and a good friend of unfinished,*
> *clumsy fingers*
> *like the undersigned scrivener's*
>
> *Carl Sandburg*
> *1   9   6   0*

Since her early school days, Virginia Pasley's hero had been Carl Sandburg; he lived and worked as a newspaperman in her own city of Chicago. Virginia became a journalist herself. Even then her path never crossed Sandburg's. Then she married Chicago newsman Fred Pasley of the *Tribune.* Like a wedding present, she had her meeting with Sandburg at last: all along, he had been one of her husband's best chums along newspaper row.

Fred died in 1951, and Virginia became one of Carl's special charges, a favorite in his court of ladies. For the rest of his life, he watched over her like a father.

I doubt if any one of Carl's friends possessed more book inscriptions from him than did Virginia Pasley. She had a bulging bookshelf of them. So I give here just a few of the more typical examples by a writer who knew the art of writing fine sentiments.

In *Remembrance Rock,* the only book Carl inscribed both to Virginia and her husband, and curiously, the only one dated, Carl wrote:

> *For Fred and Virginia Pasley*
>
> *who know issues*
> *and love people*
> *and will not get*
> *lost herein*
>
> *affectionately*
>
> *Carl Sandburg*
> *1   9   4   8*

Sandburg's inscription in *Complete Poems* is a long one, perhaps in lieu of a letter owed:

> *Virginia—first read*
> *the notes for a Preface, then*
> *one by one the 861 poems*
> *good and bad, and then if you love me*
> *a million bushels or even one*
> *thousand bushels, then across*
> *the next million years, thru*
> *all my reincarnations, I will*
> *remember your name, your*
> *face, your voice, saying you are*
> *worthy of deep love, high blessings*
>
> > *Carl Sandburg*

This whimsical message to Virginia in *Always The Young Strangers* was written most probably in 1953:

> *For Virginia Pasley*
>
> *who is always young*
> *but never no stranger*
> *to me says the scrivener*
>
> > *Carl Sandburg*

Virginia especially prized a first edition of *Rootabaga Stories,* published in 1922. The book went wherever Virginia went; she had read and reread it as a child, then as an adult aloud to her nieces and nephews. She knew many passages of the enchanting stories by heart.

When Virginia met Carl at last, she charmed him by quoting pure and simple to Sandburg the opening passage of the opening tale in *Rootabaga Stories:* "How They Broke Away to Go to the Rootabaga Country."

Carl wrote an extra-special inscription in Virginia's childhood copy of *Rootabaga Stories:*

> *It is my impression,*
> *Virginia, that you are*
> *one of those lucky-born*
> *to whom it is earlier*
> *than you think—*
>
> > *Carl*

After hearing Ethel Smith play, Carl Sandburg dubbed the tiny organist "the Poet of the Console." Thus, as between poets, they quickly found their spiritual meeting ground. But not too much time passed before there developed, too, a healthy kissing relationship. *"Chee!"* Ethel exclaimed one day, reeling into our kitchen just after Carl had bussed her soundly. "If only he were a little younger . . . or I a little older!"

Ethel was high up on Carl's "must see" list, but socializing was not always possible when he was in town. At such times, there was always the telephone. A few days after one of Carl's telephone visits, Ethel received *The People, Yes,* inscribed:

> *Ethel Smith*
>
> > *whose kiss via phone*
> > *is by no means equally*
> > *repaid by this book—*
> > *yet you are a beautiful*
> > *child of the people & I*
> > *am among those who*
> > *love you and your art*
> >
> > > *Carl Sandburg*
> > > *1 9 5 6*

and again, in a copy of *Remembrance Rock:*

> *For E. S.*
>
> *Who may detect herein*
> *both meaning and music—*
> *& here is admiration*
> *for your genius, wit,*
> *and follies—also here*
> *a loving heart*
>
> > *Carl Sandburg*
> > *1 9 5 7*

In 1952, Carl visited the antique-laden Victorian mansion of Rose and Albert Augustine on New York's Central Park West. Cradled in his arm was a bulky brown package containing Sandburg's *Complete Poems* written between the years 1910 and 1950, containing the 861 poems mentioned in Virginia Pasley's inscription. Correction—862: the inscription on the flyleaf was yet another poem. The Augustine collection consisted mainly of stringed instruments: lutes, archelutes, theorbos, harpsichords, violas da Gamba, and early guitars of every type. Remembering this stunning array of ancient instruments, Sandburg inscribed in the book:

For Rose and Albert Augustine with thanks for the memorable hours in your rooms where antique stringed instruments remember good players they knew and are pleased to be liberated from bad players

Carl Sandburg

1 9 5 2

Sandburg saw the Stecklers for the first time in the mid-1950s during a party at Henderson Place. Olga Steckler was everybody's princess, and like any red-blooded American boy, Sandburg was immediately taken with her stunning looks, her grace, and her charm. After a time of ogling Olga, he looked about the room, curious to understand better the young man with the stuff to have won such a beauty.

Ah, there he was, standing on his head, singing "Be my Love" as lustily as Mario Lanza had ever sung it, right side up. Of course! How could the fair Olga resist so fascinating a man? Sandburg saw what it was that Olga saw in Len: a madcap greatness. Instantly, Len took his place in Carl's pantheon of fabled heroes and heroines, eminently qualifying for the leading character in a *New Rootabaga Stories*—if ever Carl got to write another book of such tales.

When Carl next saw the Stecklers, it was with a book under his arm, signifying his complete admiration. He wrote in *Complete Poems:*

For Len and Olga Steckler

Who sing, act, and dance,
impersonate, attitudinize,
& sometimes pluck stars
from the night sky—

Carl Sandburg

1 9 5 7

In 1964, after more than seven decades as one of America's most peripatetic writers, Sandburg at eighty-four was tired. His rugged health and keen memory at last began to yield to the tug of time. Finally he gathered his shawls and leg warmers about him and settled down for good at his home on Connemara Farm, Flat Rock, North Carolina—hundreds of miles from the fun, friendships, follies, and folderols of the guitar people in New York. One line of communication stayed open and at the New York end of it was big Joe Wershba.

The sun had already set for Sandburg. Only a soft afterglow remained in his firmament before the night would close in. Paula Sandburg was firm in her resolve to make those last few years a time of rest and reflection for her husband of five and a half decades. Of Carl's myriad contacts in New York, Paula chose Joe as the liaison between Flat Rock and the big city. He had visited Connemara several times; he was one of the first the Sandburg family had met, liked, and immediately trusted right down the line. To learn anything about Carl which was reliable, we New Yorkers got the latest from Joe.

Joe and Carl first met in the early 1950s, in the early days of TV, when Edward R. Murrow's "See It Now" was one of the best shows on the new medium. Joe was a field reporter for Murrow, and he rehearsed with Sandburg for a forthcoming show on February 10, 1952 from Lincoln Memorial commemorating, of course, Lincoln's birthday.

The broadcast was live—a "first" from the Memorial and a "first" for Sandburg on the Murrow show. Following the broadcast, Wershba, with Sandburg in tow, went to the home of his CBS colleague Eric Sevareid in Washington. In the course of their visit with the commentator there came a call from Sevareid's nephew, who had just seen the show at home and expressed awe at Sandburg's readings from *The People, Yes* standing on the top steps of the Memorial. He said: "I couldn't tell Sandburg from the statue of Lincoln. Which was the statue?"

Carl's inscription to Joe in *Remembrance Rock* is an eloquent commemoration of the day they first met:

For Joe Wershba
the battling kid, the swift panther, the old reliable, the seeker, the relentless hunter of the American Dream, peculiar amalgam of artist & executive, on

Old Troubadour

*Feb. 10, 1952 gifted director and prompter of the long undersigned scrivener
of this long journey of the American People, which it behooves JW to read
on account of he is here & there & hither and yon amid the pages—*

Carl Sandburg

There. Does the reader read affection, trust, and dependence in
those lines? Paula Sandburg would; they were lines that characterized
the communication lines she entrusted to Joe from 1964 to 1967.

Shirley Wershba, like her husband Joe, was a television journalist
and in Carl's court of ladies, a dark-eyed favorite. Carl spoke of the
Wershbas very often. He relished just saying their names—"Joe and
Shirley Wershba"—a rare and felicitous arrangement of syllables, free
of hissing sibilant or caustic consonant. Sandburg said the names,
starting slowly and softly from deep down in his throat, releasing
them mellifluously and caressingly into the air.

The Wershbas, of all Sandburg's inscription recipients that I have
searched out, are the only ones who possess the rare *Le Peuple, Oui*, a
French translation of *The People, Yes*. Though the small volume is
inscribed to the parents, son Don and daughter Randy are in Carl's
thoughts.

For Joe and Shirley Wershba
so the children
can be learnt
French

Carl

Dolores Wilson was the acknowledged prima donna of The Silly
Center Opera Company. Our local and immediate rival for her
services was the Metropolitan, downtown a ways. It was Dolores to
whom Sandburg wrote his most sentimental "love" letters, for he
loved sopranos.

My friendship with Sandburg began when he had entered the stage
of life known statistically as "old age" and poetically as "the twilight
of life." He was seventy. If he was in the twilight of life, then it was a
long one indeed—like the gloaming of an Arctic summer.

In those days, I knew some of the women who fascinated Carl. All
of them, as might be expected, were considerably younger than he. It
was not Carl's fame with its attendant influence which won the ladies.

He exuded true charm and his feelings about women were those of a boy, idealistic and highminded. This flattering attention, and refreshing old-world gallantry was not lost on the women he met everywhere he went, especially the younger ones, surrounded as they were by new-world young men, aloof, effete, cynical, and too tired for anything like the old-fashioned chase of a man after maid until she caught him. They knew the routine and were having none of that romantic razzle-dazzle.

Sandburg was always attracted to women with accomplishments in the arts. Any natural beauty that came with the talent was an added bonus, and Dolores Wilson was generously endowed with talent, beauty, and more. She also had humor, vitality, and intelligence. Sandburg became her white-haired knight in shining blue serge. Of course he gave her books, writing into each one of them messages of love.

Someday, perhaps, a scholar of romantic writing will put together a collection of classic love letters, calling it *Great Love Letters of All Time,* and Carl Sandburg will not only be the best represented qualitatively, but also quantitatively, for he wrote love letters of many kinds. The ribbon binding them together was honesty.

It was early in 1908 that Sandburg began to show his extraordinary gifts as a persuasive writer of love letters. He was sending off a series of them at the time to a pretty young school teacher he'd just met in Milwaukee. These letters gradually moved toward a specific target: marriage. Carl's aim was perfect, and his letters helped win the fair Paula. But they did not stop there. Wherever he might be on his absences from home, he wrote as if to rewin his girl, reaffirming his love. So it went for sixty years. Only his death stopped the flow. And only Paula received that kind of a love letter. But he never stopped writing love letters of other kinds. In fact, he hardly ever wrote any which were *not* love letters. If he wrote one to you, it was for *you* to know the kind of love he was professing, how deep it went, how committed he was to it. And if you read him correctly, you knew where you stood.

Dolores Wilson had no trouble quickly reading and absorbing *Remembrance Rock,* the long journey, the long haul, as Carl called his first and only novel. A fat book was no more intimidating to her than a fat part in an opera or a musical. She had the training and discipline for concentration and retention. But she wouldn't have needed those skills in any case. Her pride in knowing the great writer and her desire to know him better through his writings were incentives that made the going child's play for her. But more than anything else she was eager to find the meaning of Carl's message in his inscription to her, to meet the "lone hearts" akin to her own:

A long journey here, dear
Dolores. May you meet lone
hearts akin to your own
brightly deep and luminous
heart. So says your scrivener

Carl Sandburg
1   9   6   0

Carl found Dolores luminous, and so began calling her "Loom," not the least reason being his keen Scandinavian relish of the "oo" sound. He rolled it over around his palate like a tasty morsel of smorgasbord.

Sooner or later, a new friend of Sandburg's would find on his doorstep one memorable day the Sandburg bonanza: the six-volume biography of Abraham Lincoln. Dolores Wilson passed her test with flying colors and in record time; her six volumes arrived soon after Carl had met her on the night she triumphed in "Lucia" with The Silly Center Opera Company. Carl promised an inscription at the first opportunity, and it came in mid-September 1960, after the Broadway opening of Norman Corwin's show, *The World of Carl Sandburg,* at the Henry Miller Theatre.

Dolores was Carl's companion for the evening, and after the show guided him to one of her favorite night clubs, the Upstairs Downstairs, for a snack. His presence duly feted and his hunger sated, Carl saw it as time to escort the lady home. She saw it as proper to ask him in for a nightcap and almost before he was seated and relaxed, with nightcap at elbow, glad to be away from the fuss and feathers of the Upstairs Downstairs, Dolores set his Lincoln volumes before him.

Abraham Lincoln was deeply a part of Carl Sandburg's world; Corwin's work contained many evocations of the Great Emancipator. Now, seated before his story of Lincoln's monumental life, Carl picked out one of the volumes and turned the pages unerringly to his description of the death of Lincoln and its aftermath, the long railroad funeral cortege and the stunned sadness of the people along the way. Carl read aloud until finally his voice trailed off, and only a faint echo of his voice remained in the room.

Into the book from which he had read so copiously, Sandburg wrote sparsely:

Dolores = please keep me in your thoughts often = you are one of earth's brightest, says this scrivener—

Carl

In 1953, we saw the first installment of the Sandburg saga, his autobiography *Always The Young Strangers,* which took our young stranger from crib to college, just twenty years of his life. The book ran to 436 solidly packed pages, 195,000 words—and Sandburg had barely *begun* to live.

Of this, Carl seemed wearily aware. His inscription in the book he gave to Dolores reflects it. And how well in so few words does he express his sensibility of the job ahead, the flood of words yet to come, awaiting their turn . . .

Dolores

*& so much
not told at
all—not at
all!*

Carl

In the summer of 1960, Sandburg wrote his friend Alvin W. Dreier of the *Chicago Tribune:* "I am going to back Kennedy as against Nixon, but I have taken an oath not to tear my shirt." Then he took off with fellow North Carolinian, writer Harry Golden, to stump for the golden boy of Boston and keep his vow. He came away from every rally, every campaign speech, without a tear in his shirt. But there was a tearing at his heart, for he was saying goodbye for a long time, to friends and well-wishers in New York.

His last stop would be Hollywood, where he was helping George Stevens tell the story of Jesus' life on film, in *The Greatest Story Ever*

Told. Along the way, he stumped for JFK. After arriving in the cinema capital, Carl made frequent one-night stands with Golden in nearby cities and communities.

If laughter comes easy to one, as it did to Sandburg, so then do tears. More poignantly so when the poet is over eighty and goodbyes are not tossed off as lightly as when he was a sprightly seventy.

When Carl headed west, he left an inscribed copy of his *Sandburg Range* for Dolores Wilson:

> *Loom*
> > *Don't forget the near*
> > *departure evening of*
> > *tears in duo*
>
> > > *Carl*

But the odds held with their old tenacity. At eighty-two Carl Sandburg was never more alive and well and ambulatory, even staking out new boundaries. He was a journalist, teller of children's tales for grownups, collector of Americana and Americans, troubadour, guitarist, co-founder of The Silly Center Opera Company, jokesmith, celebrity, poet, essayist, biographer, historian, infantryman, goatherder and breeder, political campaigner—and now, a Hollywood scriptwriter at work on a story about a man who would like to have known the pleasure of his company.

23

Links to Lincoln: A Walk in Carl Schurz Park

THE FOOT OF EAST 86TH STREET, New York City, steps invitingly into the mouth of Carl Schurz Park, commonly referred to as our mayor's backyard. Gracie Mansion, sitting snugly inside the 87th Street entrance has housed New York's mayors since Fiorello LaGuardia moved in as the first official occupant in 1933.

Sandburg's curiosity about our little park and its huge river below had been aroused from the first day he knew they were there. He liked the idea of looking down on a river he had heard was not a real river, but a deep salt water strait. On hearing the name of the park, a twitch of pink ear and flash of Scandinavian blue eye signalled we were in for a walk—in good weather, I hoped.

The good weather passed relentlessly into a very cold day in 1960. Seeing the thermometer had dropped to ten degrees, I decided to give myself a day in—one of the privileges of being a free-lance, work-at-home artist. My smug complacency at not having to leave the house was suddenly shattered by the ringing of the doorbell—not the kind you're saved by, but the one that tolls the knell of a day in departing. Its distinctive sound could only signify Carl Sandburg's technique at the button.

"Show me your park." The well-bundled Sandburg in the doorway had no intention of removing so much as the tip of his hat. I had no choice. With misgivings and much remonstrance, I bundled and scarved myself against the icy winds and joined my intrepid friend.

The park was deserted of sensible people, but not of insensible ghosts. We met our first at the Eighty-sixth Street entrance. Just inside the gate Carl Sandburg and Carl Schurz (two C. S.'s) were meeting before a bronze plaque, some 20″ × 30″, riveted to a smoothed-out rectangle of Manhattan rock. In raised block letters, it read:

CARL SCHURZ
Soldier, Statesman, Philanthropist
1829–1906

Not until I'd encountered the name of Carl Schurz in Carl Sandburg's *The War Years* had I any idea who this "soldier, statesman, philanthropist" might be—how he came to rate a park in New York City named for him. Even General Friederich Wilhelm von Steuben, the Revolutionary War hero, does not enjoy such recognition. Except for an annual parade sponsored by the Deutcher-American folk of Yorkville, the uniforms, bunting, lederhosen, meerschaum pipes and oompah bands go back into mothballs until the next year. But Schurz—he's always there, east a piece, rain or shine, season to season.

Sandburg looked steadily, attentively at the plaque, his ear cocked. Now and then, he nodded assent. Then he turned to go. We made for the shallow steps leading up to the promenade overlooking the river. Not until we were at some distance—as if out of earshot of the plaque—did Carl speak again. Tossing his head rearward, he said: "Lincoln spoke his inner thoughts to that man." The story of Schurz and his involvement with Lincoln and the Civil War is in *The War Years* and much of the author's historical data and sidelights on the war of the states and the political intrigues contained in the book were from the actual writings and memoirs of Schurz, a journalist who had fled Germany to escape arrest for insurrectionary activity, coming to the U.S. via France and England in 1852. It was to this German immigrant of revolutionary ideas and wild visage that Lincoln poured out his despair and disillusionment in 1864 when nominated for a second term. He was crushed and discouraged by the political climate pervading Washington, and the jealousy and desertion of men who were once close friends. They were now urging him to withdraw from the race, though he had been unanimously nominated by his party. What hurt most, Lincoln told Schurz, was the accusation that he lusted for power, and was hurting the common cause.

Now we had gained the top of the steps, and despite their ease of ascent, the puffs of condensed air of my breathing were three to Sandburg's one. Our sudden emergence into the free, unobstructed blasts of wind atop the promenade twisted my face into instant mummification, and Sandburg's into a pink, mischievous grin. "I wonder if the people up the street know," he said, gesturing toward Yorkville, "that Carl Schurz, like their General von Steuben, was also a general. Lincoln appointed him to head the Third Division in the Civil War." Then he looked upward and peered closely into a gray cloud—his teleprompter in the sky. There he found other names of generals in the Union Army, of German birth or extraction. This sent me later that day to *The War Years*. And there they were: Bushbeck, Von Steinwehr, Von Schluembach; and last, but the most, Schimmelpfennig, which, I remembered, Carl pronounced with particular relish to the last Teutonic guttural.

We strode across the walk to a railing of unusual design running the full length of the promenade. Its uniqueness was marked by a sharp, inward curve from its knee-high base of concrete. This is what stood as a deterrent against plunges, voluntary or involuntary, into the rushing river fifty feet below. Carl leaned over the odd barrier; now he was looking down into this river, at last keeping his date with it. And in a few minutes, he would be shaking hands with another ghost of the past, this one at a somewhat higher eye level than Schurz, but closer in time to Carl.

Just to the left of us stood a thick steel pole, set into a block of concrete and rising to a height of some ten feet. It was topped by a plaque, vertically set, in approximately the same dimensions as the Schurz piece. But this metalwork was of a different motif, a bas-relief with the background cut out, leaving a border. Within it, we saw the silhouette of a man in profile walking vigorously northward against a stylized design of the Manhattan skyline. Plain block letters spelled out JOHN FINLEY WALK. The cut-out figure, the skyline and the lettering had as sky, the sky itself. Its color as seen through the openings of the plaque was dead-gloom gray.

Sandburg gazed reverently at the cut-out on high as if it was an icon; its emotional impact was the greater for the suddenness of its appearance, and so soon in our tour of the park. Carl Sandburg had known he would find Carl Schurz in Carl Schurz Park, but stumbling unexpectedly upon John Finley, boyhood hero of his Galesburg days, left him speechless. When he found his tongue he said, as if talking to himself "John Finley—John Huston Finley—walkin' as usual . . . when I first saw him, he was walkin' . . . ."

In his autobiography *Always The Young Strangers,* which covers the first twenty years of his life, Sandburg tells of seeing Finley on a street in Galesburg. This was almost six decades before seeing Finley cut out in bronze against a New York skyline. Here, I suspected, was another link with Lincoln; but as I learned in *Strangers,* a link once removed. At age twenty-nine Finley became president of Knox College in Galesburg—the youngest such administrator then in the United States. It was as a great admirer of Lincoln that Finley put Knox College on the map, hosting several of the Lincoln-Douglas debates.

But the walking man above us was not the Finley of the year 1892, in Galesburg, Illinois, head down, in deep thought as he passes young milkman Carl Sandburg. Our Finley of Finley Walk in the Carl Schurz Park, New York, 1960, was, of course, an older man, but a very exuberant figure. His head was high, scarf a-flying in the wind, stride vigorous, and carrying a cane; a man of purpose, going somewhere, and his destination was the very spot from which he had started. It was a once-a-year ritual during the decade 1920–1930, when he was editor of *The New York Times,* for Finley to walk the perimeter of Manhattan Island—in one day!

As my attention shifted, Sandburg to Finley, Finley to Sandburg, my artist's eye searched for something I saw in the Finley figure that reminded me of Sandburg. I was suddenly struck by a remarkable phenomenon, at once eerie, yet somehow logical: the two were look-alikes. At least in profile the resemblance was amazing, not only in their facial contours, but also in leg gesture—the same baggy pants, the stubby-toed feet, and of course, the flying scarf. Even the fedora sported by Finley was not unlike the style of Sandburg's hats. I mentioned all these points of similarity to Sandburg. "The only thing missing," I said, "is the walking stick." "I don't carry one in the city," he answered, "but I guess I'd need one if I had to walk clear around it. But I got a lotta sticks at home for takin' those mountain trails around Connemara."

Now we were approaching Eighty-fourth Street, known chicly at this last block of the park's south end as Gracie Square. Carl glanced at the river running counter to our direction as we trudged on. "Slow goin', ain't it?" he said. "Well, after all, we're buckin' the tide."

Reaching the end, Sandburg eagerly scanned the upper floors of one of the buildings. "Somewhere up there," he said, "André lives." Kostelanetz, I knew he meant. And I knew too, that another Lincoln association beckoned.

The Lincoln-Sandburg-Kostelanetz connection was no misty evocation of the past, but an annual event more palpable, audible, dramatic, and publicly involved. It was Lincoln in words and music— Sandburg saying the words, Kostelanetz baton-cueing him; and an orchestra the size of a brigade playing the thrilling score of Aaron Copland's "Lincoln Portrait," commissioned in patriotic fervor by Maestro Kostelanetz himself. This was a ritual with the little Russian emigre; on or around a Memorial Day or a Lincoln's birthday, in whatever concert hall of any city of the U.S. he found himself, the Copland work was the *pièce de resistance* of the program.

"This is as far as we can go this end; er—shall we head for home now?" I asked wistfully through turned up collar and multiple scarves. "Let's go to the other end," Carl said brightly. "Oh, come on," he added, seeing my anguished wince, "it'll be easier this time, goin' with the tide."

We found the path from Gracie Mansion leading back toward the river, regained the John Finley Walk, and continued our explorations north. Ahead of us was a pier and on it, a low, red bungalow, the headquarters, a sign said, of Marine Company Number 5 of the New York City Fire Department. Tied up at the uptown side of the pier, a large fireboat rolled lazily at its now taut, now slack hawsers. It measured some 100 feet, with a super-structure of white and the hull, of course, a fire-engine red. All of the brass nozzles gleamed brightly, even in the pale winter light. Large letters in gold-leaf across the length of the cabin proclaimed the name of the jaunty craft: SENATOR ROBERT WAGNER.

Sandburg's admiration for the father of our then mayor, father of the social security system of the U.S. and the National Labor Relations Act of 1937 was deep. Carl ran his eye appreciatively along the gracefully curved hull of the fireboat. "Schurz had the same revolutionary spirit," he said. "What Schurz stood for in Germany, Wagner stood for here—wage-labor, and not slave-labor . . . uh, uh . . ." He hesitated a moment. "I guess you could say that Lincoln preserved the Union . . . ," a brief pause; Sandburg's timing was worthy of a Jack Benny—"but Wagner preserved the unions."

Although I had returned from the petrified park somewhat of a glacier, I was thankful that when I tried to back out of the walk, Carl had not backed down. It was inevitable; the ghosts were expecting him out there. This and no other day was the day, and with or without me, he would have kept his appointments.

One day in 1968 I entered Carl Schurz Park to check on a detail or two regarding the plaque inside the gate at the Eighty-sixth Street entrance. Only the bare rock remained. The plaque, since 1910 an integral part of the typically schistose Manhattan outcropping, weighed well over 100 solid bronze pounds—and it was gone! "Presumed stolen," as the Monuments Division of the Parks Department of New York City ruefully informed me later that day. It would be replaced, however, I was assured. The audaciousness of the thieves amazed me. This was no mere snatch-and-run job, but one requiring heavy tools, like a crowbar and a hacksaw, at least—tools which must have set off a clank and screech in the night, not to mention that the caper was performed under the good lighting from nearby lampposts. But performed only under the eye of God, it seems, for until I informed the Parks Department, nobody, including the police, was even aware that the plaque was missing. Since it had been some time since I had actually entered the park, it might well have been stolen long before.

As late as Christmas week, 1986, now as I finish *Old Troubadour,* I still see no replaquement. The leveled area of the rock into which it had been riveted—for the first few months of a lighter hue, like the square on a wall where once a picture hung—has given up waiting and taken on the safe coloration of its mother rock.

Replaced, the man said. He meant with a new one, of course, for the old one can never be replaced—not the one where two famous C. S.'s, with links to Lincoln, met one cold winter's day twenty-five years ago.

Goodbye to Henderson Place

ACROSS FROM US ON NARROW Henderson Place stood a squat, homely relic of old-world charm, the Misericordia Hospital, so far gone in decay that to expend a single sou more on the repair of a single rusty pipe would be like throwing money into the sewer. Its days were numbered, we began to hear. We shuddered even to speculate on what new urbanality would replace it. For three years, we had enjoyed the almost cloistered silence of the small, off-to-one-side street, a silence shared appreciatively by Carl Sandburg in 1957 and 1958 on his two protracted visits with us. But now, the New York building boom was finding our range. Real estate interests would soon draw bead on this choice site. Their diagnosis: the land was fine and could remain; but the eighty-year-old hospital had to go. From the ancient red-brick rubble would be erected two high-rise brick cooperatives the color of New York soot.

It was Carl Sandburg's pleasure to stand at his top-floor window for many minutes at a time and read the street below him, taking in the architectural detail of the hospital nearly as old as himself. Especially did he enjoy observing the tiny Sisters of the Misericordia Order, their shining, scrubbed, pink faces ovaled in black and white headdresses, their voluminous habiliments ballooning in the special breezes of Henderson Place. He marveled, too, at their skillful maneuvering of the long, black hospital station wagons in and out of the narrow parking spaces.

It saddened us to see the hospital go, with its black-robed nuns and its white-uniformed young interns. The entrance for emergency cases was at a perfect ninety degrees cross-over from our side of the street, twenty yards away at the most. This just-a-jump-away distance was of great comfort to us always; its instant accessibility might spell the difference in a life-or-death emergency. Though the hospital building was of mid-Victorian vintage, its physicians, nurses, methods, and equipment were up to the minute in modernity. I must confess, that with an octogenarian in the house, a world-renowned figure at that, a guest for whose well-being I held myself responsible, that emergency entrance was a steadying presence. Praise be, we never used it. Sandburg's heart and digestion were sound; and so were his liver, blood pressure, lungs, eyes, ears, nose, throat, and sense of humor.

We were besieged by the crash of tumbling walls; the blast of dynamite; the shattering clatter of pneumatic drills; the shouts and profanities of an army of laborers; the explosive chug of bulldozer and steam shovel; the clank of concrete mixers; the exhaust, the soot; plumbing dislodged and ominous cracks appeared in our walls from extra-charged dynamite blasts; debris caught in strong winds and blew clear across the street to our roof, clogging gutters and the drains and starting leaks in our ceilings from the collected pools of water.

The news of the havoc on Henderson Place reached Carl Sandburg all the way down in Flat Rock, North Carolina.

"It comes reported," he wrote me, "that Henderson Place is a shambles, meaning it is either an abattoir or a slaughterhouse."

I went into first degree N.Y. Building Boom Shell Shock. In such extremis, I answered Carl's letter, detailing my anguish, pain by pain, adding that the pain that really stabbed me was realizing that the shambles on Henderson Place precluded for the next few years, when a feather quilt of silence would again cover it, any extended stays he might have in mind. Even an overnight visit would be out of the question, late sleeper that he was. For promptly at 7:30 every morning, the first dynamite charge would be set off, blasting away a chunk of Manhattan from its bedrock and Sandburg from his bed.

My impassioned letter to Carl drew a soothing answer of sweet medicine: flattery. He wrote: "Your sentences about the sesquipedalian demolition across the street, the never-ending goddam götter-dämmerung—these were keen and musical reporting."

During the many months of the "goddam götterdämmerung," Sandburg found havens with other friends in the city or he went to The Royalton Hotel. But the guitar people continued to gather on Henderson Place as always, at night, of course, when the raging beast across the way was in slumber.

In July 1960, Sandburg was called to Hollywood by George Stevens to work on the script of *The Greatest Story Ever Told*. That assignment completed, Carl began to slow down. He was now past eighty-two, traveling less and sticking close to home. Though we saw him again at one function or another, he never saw Henderson Place again. Had he braved Henderson Place at any time over those months, nothing could have restrained me from rushing to my plaque maker's and ordering one of his larger bronzes for my front door, to read in bold, raised letters:

CARL SANDBURG COULDN'T SLEEP HERE: 1959–1960

Carl didn't forget Henderson Place, though, even while living in the perfumed air of Beverly Hills. Taking time off from work on Stevens's script, he wrote me a letter. It arrived on a cold, gloomy December day. It came as a warm gleam of California sunshine. If his balmy surroundings had succeeded in working their lazy allure on Sandburg, his letters gave evidence of no such surrender.

"I miss the fellowship with the guitarists," he wrote. "I miss hearing you play that Mexican Song Number 2. But when I am somewhat footloose again, I will be haunting the premises of a house on which I say blessings."

Forgettery

THIS IS MY TIME OF LIFE when I can best write a memoir of Carl Sandburg.

I am grateful to Sandburg for having lived as long as he did. Now that I have attained a more reasonable age parity with him, I can write about him sympathetically and empathetically, as a fellow oldster rather than an awed and eager youngster, dancing attendance upon him worshipfully, but now with understanding of the problems that wait like thieves in the nighttime of life.

When I first met Sandburg in 1948, he was already a venerable seventy, sound of wind and limb, in his right and brilliant mind, especially that compartment of it which regulated the memory. For years, never could I count any serious diminution in the assets of his memory bank. In fact, he could perform feats of memory that would be staggering even in a man half his age.

As the years passed, I dreamily assumed that although Sandburg must of course leave us one day, it would not be through the prosaic process of brain, tissue, or organic deterioration, as comes to all men. No, Carl would go as a giant tree would go, falling suddenly and mysteriously in the forest while still in its fullest foliage, as if nature said, "Enough. You are relieved of duty. You had grown so tall, you were beginning to block the view of other growing trees."

This was the image of indestructible Carl that I took with me to the Waldorf Hotel on January 6, 1963, when double good fortune was celebrated: Sandburg's eighty-fifth birthday and the publication of his new volume of poems *Honey and Salt.* The party, of course, was given by Harcourt Brace and World, Sandburg's publishers since 1919. No expense was spared; it was a top-burner Waldorf dinner, and the 108 guests included notables in artistic, intellectual, academic, and political life from playwright Albee to sculptor Zorach.

It had been months since I'd last seen Sandburg. As I watched him in the distance at the center of the speakers' table, I thought he had never looked healthier or ruddier, or more like that wise, old, snowy-haired Norse king who climbed into Herr Bauer's Number One chair for the epoch-making haircut five years before. Straight as an arrow he sat, clad in his dark suit and bow tie, as close to evening clothes as he ever got.

He looked somehow detached, as if something of his essence had been extinguished. If anybody had suggested that the figure of Sandburg seated in the place of honor was a clever duplicate of the poet, I would have believed it.

Dinner and speeches were over. The speeches were short, for the most part, Sandburg's being the shortest, mildest, most perfunctory I had ever heard him make. He did not even hurl his regular blast at the "obscura-a-antists." Now the guests, each with a complimentary copy of *Honey and Salt,* lined up for autographs and whatever else Sandburg had for them, greetings cool or warm; embraces; kisses, exchanges or private words. They passed before his table, Terry and I among them.

Terry's turn came just ahead of me. Carl received the proffered book and accommodatingly opened at the flyleaf. To my surprise and dismay, his first notice of her was almost blank, a slow frown, and a "You look familiar" look. Then he leaned over the better to see her face, and nodded.

With a "haw" of self-annoyance, he asked: "Just how do you spell your name again?"

Terry betrayed surprise only by a flicker of her eyes and a deep sadness, recognizing that asking for the spelling of a name is a transparent device to hide total blankness of the name itself. But quickly, she snapped up, saying brightly: "Oh, any way you like. Terry can be spelled either with a 'y' or an 'i.'"

It was her device to ease Carl's embarrassment, though he had written her name countless times in the past, and always with the correct ending, "y." Slowly, in his simple block handwriting which had remained constant over the years, Sandburg wrote: "Terry—1963—Love—Carl."

Would Carl also forget me? I trembled to think that the same mortifying experience might be in store for me—ME—his guitar pal of so many years! I quickly formulated a plan that would give him and me a minimum of pain in such an event. My turn would come, and Carl would peer closely into my face, and ask: "Just how do you spell your name again?" And manfully, betraying no indignation, I would answer: "With only one 'g' on the end . . ." More, I would even spell my name out fully: "G-R-E-G."

But my own memory was deserting me. I had forgotten—and in only a space of minutes—that my name was clearly written on the flyleaf where Sandburg would write his autograph. I had signed it under a drawing I made of him from my table during the speeches. I had drawn other prominent figures as well—Edward Steichen and Mahalia Jackson, who were among the guests seated with Sandburg at the center table. They were just beyond Carl, and I hoped they would autograph my quick sketches of them as I passed down the line.

I handed the open book up to Carl at his slightly elevated place at the table. The smile he had for me was a leftover of the smile that he had not fully spent on Terry. As he inspected my drawing, it faded entirely.

"Do I look like that?" he asked coldly. Then, without waiting for my excuse, he wrote, snapped the book shut, and handed it back to me. I moved forward, head down, fumbling to find the flyleaf, anxious to see what warm personal message Sandburg had written for his old guitar pal. Sandburg had played it safe—safer even than he had with Terry; he may or may not have seen my signature. In any event, he omitted any salutation, signing the page simply "Carl Sandburg."

At Virginia Pasley's some time after the Sandburg birthday dinner, I mentioned my sorrow at Carl's memory lapse and its alarming suddenness.

"Suddenness?" Virginia said. "Just a minute, and I'll show you something." She opened a desk drawer and scooped up a handful of letters, extracted one and handed it to me. It was a short note from Sandburg to her, postmarked Flat Rock, North Carolina. It read:

July 2 1959

Dear Virginia:

I have lost Gregory's address. I can tell a taxi driver how to get there and unless considerably stupified, I could walk there on a dark night and on entering, find my way without switching on a light. I even know the house number. Tell me why I should forget the name of the shortest street in the largest city of our dear country? . . . Enclosed should go forward to Gregory d'Alessio, our cherished guitar pal. I am not proud of my forgettery nor do I hang my head in shame . . . Salutations, love and blessings.

Carl

Virginia pointed to the date atop the letter. Almost four years ago! As early as that, and perhaps even earlier, forgettery was beginning to knock on the door of Sandburg's memory chamber. That Henderson Place was a victim, of all places, was amazing even to the forgetter; and he could have enlarged even more on the stubbornness of his forgettery by pointing out that when homeward bound from Henderson Place, the name of the town in North Carolina he would need to head for first before he could reach Connemara Farm, Flat Rock, was Hendersonville, site of the nearest railroad station.

But thankfully, a lapse is not a loss. A candle always burns in the mind's window. Sooner or later, there is a ring of the doorbell, and it is the wandering memory come home again. A letter from Carl arrived from Hollywood in 1960. "I miss you and Terry," he wrote; "and the very walls of Henderson Place."

In 1963, André Kostelanetz beckoned to Sandburg with his baton, once again inviting him to narrate Copland's tone poem, "A Lincoln Portrait." Despite a waiting pool of professional actors eager for a crack at the prestigious assignment, Kostelanetz always gave Sandburg first refusal.

Fittingly, on Memorial Day 1963, Carl's last Lincoln tribute was a première at New York's new Lincoln Center.

The performance went very smoothly. Under the wise and understanding baton of Maestro Kostelanetz, Sandburg performed like the old amateur-pro he had become at this job, coming through with every dramatic pause and tempo change on pinpoint cue. It was a highly emotional twenty minutes that we underwent. Terry and I and all of Sandburg's friends in the audience, knowing that we were watching his farewell on this or any other stage. We saw him at eighty-five, standing straight and strong at the lectern, aglow in a soft spotlight, God letting him do yet another time this beloved work.

Now I began to wonder about Act II, which would be staged in the Green Room of the Philharmonic, where artists receive after-concert friends and other well-wishers. Without script or cue, how would he endure the backstage ordeal? Would his forgettery be hovering about his head? Whom would he remember in the receiving line; what would he remember of them?

Carl had brought the Missus up north with him this time, and his eldest daughter, Margaret. From the end of the long line where Terry and I were waiting, we could see the receiving quartet, Carl, Paula, Margaret, and Kostelanetz. Carl's white locks bobbed up and down joyfully. We could hear the hearty boom of his greetings. He was saying the name of each friend loud and clear, and when he faced Terry, he bussed and hugged her and said hers, too.

When I stood before him, my name, too, came quickly, and he said it as of old—"d'Alez-z-z-i-ohhh!" Other names within the circle of our mutual associations tumbled forth: the guitar, Segovia, *The Review*, Olga Coelho, Bobri, Henderson Place . . . ah! Henderson Place . . . its very walls and Terry and I had not been completely nudged out of his memory by inexorable forgettery.

All my life Memorial Day, in its grave and reverent dedication to the tribute and honor of the war dead, was hardly more than an abstraction to me. Now this Memorial Day in my late middle age was the most significant of them all. Gratitude dispelled my gloom and pessimism that Sandburg was perhaps not indestructible, for here he was, shaking my hand until I winced, looking as mischievous as ever, fit and ready for a long boxcar evening of bourbon, guitar, songs, and stories, as in the old days.

But those days were over. Carl immediately returned to Connemara Farm with his wife and daughter, ever-vigilant over his health. A short engagement in Tampa, followed by two more weeks in Hollywood—called back by George Stevens to help in editing *The Greatest Story Ever Told*—and Sandburg's traveling days seemed to be over. His New York friends had seen the last of him; they had better start piecing together in every precious detail Memorial Day 1963, for their *last time I saw Sandburg* memoirs. We waited and waited for other days, other occasions, other diversions when Sandburg might unexpectedly blow into town; but all we were beginning to hear about him now was his slow decline, of his spending more time in bed than out of it. So we stopped waiting and started remembering.

To see Sandburg again, you had to go to Connemara Farm, and if you were a good friend, Paula cleared the way. For over two years, I had not seen Sandburg, and I ached to hear his husky, growling, bass viol voice. Should I attempt to visit him, perhaps to hear him say my name in yet another room, his own? I actually picked up the phone one day and started the process of getting a line to Connemara for the come-ahead from Paula. In the waiting time, I remembered the cold and distant Sandburg of January 1963, and the sadness I had come away with, and the happy, miraculous contrast of the resurrected Sandburg of May 31, 1963, and my overflowing joy. What would be in store for me at Connemara? In what stage of forgettery would I find Sandburg? Would he even remember "d'Alez-z-z-iohhh" and put it into the air of his room? What new, and this time, lasting sadness might await me? Before the operator ever got to ringing the Sandburg phone, I hung up.

Let It Be Easy

AT THE AGE OF FORTY-TWO, in the midst of a full and useful, vibrant, and creative life, at the threshold of even greater achievement, Carl Sandburg gave a thought to dying. It was not of death in the abstract, but death as it should come to a specific person: himself. And he wrote out his instructions in the form of a poem, with characteristic modesty and self-effacement. *From Smoke and Steel,* 1920, the poem:

FINISH

Death comes once, let it be easy.
Ring one bell for me once, let it go at that.
Or ring no bell at all, better yet.

Sing one song if I die.
Sing John Brown's Body or Shout All Over God's Heaven.
Or sing nothing at all, better yet.

Death comes once, let it be easy.

Sandburg needn't have worried. It was. "Carl had an easy going in his sleep," Paula Sandburg wrote me a few weeks after his death on July 22, 1967.

Though he had to wait almost fifty years, his first instruction was accommodated. At his memorial service in September 1967 in Washington, his two songs were sung. His beloved guitar was played by Charlie Byrd, and President Lyndon Johnson, Archibald MacLeish, and Mark Van Doren gave eulogies. Yes, death had come easy to Sandburg, but it wasn't easy for his friends, his country, the world. He had asked for one bell or no bell at all to be rung for him; but who could stop the thousands that tolled out the news?

He died at nine o'clock on Saturday morning, July 22, 1967. At 11:40 that morning Paula Sandburg telephoned the news to Joe Wershba in New York, not to newspaperman Wershba, but to Joe, a long and trusted friend of the family, whom she could depend upon to relay the story to their many mutual friends in New York.

"It was a quiet, peaceful death," she told Wershba.

Then Paula turned to her bell-ringing duties: one bell, or no bell at all? In their mutual love for simplicity, she decided on no bell at all.

Joe wrote me: "She didn't think any fuss should be made." But big brother Edward Steichen, the more worldly one of the family, insisted that the world, and not just a group of friends, must be told.

"I agreed with Steichen, I told Mrs. Carl," Joe continued. "And after calling my office at CBS, I called my old paper, *The New York Post;* then Herb Mitgang at the *Times;* then the AP and UPI. Then I called the White House, and left word for Press Secretary George Christman and Mrs. Johnson that Carl had died and that the president would probably want to issue a statement. He did, later that day."

The news first came to me the day after—Sunday—over bedside radio. Of course, it was not unexpected, and Carl's actual death was almost anticlimactic. The last two years of his life had been a slow, steady drifting toward the horizon; now, he had slipped over it and out of sight. I was not profoundly shaken as the details of the story came over the radio at my pillow; in fact, I did not wholly accept the news. I believed it, of course, but I was not ready to close the book on my old guitar pal. He was not dead to me yet; my own personal last rites remained to be performed and in a way unique among the bereaved.

Still in pajamas, I went to my studio and rooted out every sketchbook, every portfolio stashed away in drawers, closets, and shelves, and poked around for every drawing of Carl that I'd ever made during the nineteen years that I'd known him. I found to my satisfaction a score or more of them. Among the lot were some that I hardly remembered making.

The drawings were spread out before me like a game of solitaire. I did not merely look at them; I looked into them—deep into the flat line-and-tone representations of Carl Sandburg which I had come to make so easily, so quickly—even absentmindedly. (Would that my hand were as knowing on the guitar!) I found things in the drawings before me that only my fingers remembered, and I was never more grateful for the gift of this skill, or more aware of how well it served me, would always serve me.

More than painting or any other art expression, I love drawings. The need to make a drawing comes suddenly upon an artist. He can be thinking of anything from his laundry bill to Raquel Welch, and suddenly he is drawing a flower or a frog. A drawing is a modest, sincere expression, as completely stripped of all pretention as a private entry into a personal diary. It is free of the bravura dramatics of a painting, which is the artist's public performance, the thing he does which he will allow you to see. If you find the painting of Watteau dismissible as too sweet and cloying, give him another chance; look for his drawings.

Yes. I love drawings. My own are no exceptions. Particularly, do I love my own drawings. Of all the mementos I have accumulated in my lifetime, no one is richer in nostalgic associations or more stimulating to my sensory memory than a simple drawing of anything. Though it may be fragmentary, the entire *mise en scène* from which I extracted it is instantly evoked. No other vehicle can take me down memory lane with more pinpointed poignancy.

I have photographs galore of Sandburg; my studio walls are covered with them, none that I ever took, however. I never pointed a camera at him. Nor did I ever ask him to "sit" for me. How did I draw him? On the fly. Why did I draw him? Because he was there. I worked quietly, often without his knowledge, as he went about his business around our house: phoning, writing, singing, playing the guitar, reading, always within touching, bourbon-whiff and cigar smoke distance from me. If I could get away with it, I would keep the drawing from him. My anxiety over committing an invasion of his privacy was as over-fastidious as it was needless. Sandburg always knew when I was drawing him and always demanded to see the results, saying without fail, "Say, do I really look like that?" and remembering each one.

In late 1960, he heard that I'd turned my first floor at Henderson Place into an art gallery, and assumed mistakenly that among the pictures on exhibit and for sale would be the drawings I had made of him in the past. He quickly wrote me: "I would request that you do not sell any of the drawings you have made of me till I have had a chance to bid on them."

But the drawings were not for sale—even to him. Thus on the day I learned of his death, the drawings were paying off as I wanted them to. I rejoice that I resisted offers of money for them, including Carl's. For these records of a living Sandburg kept him alive for me as I gazed fondly and tenderly upon each one.

For a long time, I sat before the spread of drawings, remembering, resurrecting, and I began to see that there was a lot more remembering to be done. It had not yet crossed my mind that I should *write* my memoir of Sandburg. Although at my fingertips, scores of stories and anecdotes known only to me were itching to be told, but the itch was not to set fingers upon typewriter keys as a scrivener. That was not my trade. Instead, I wanted to grab a pencil, anything that would make a line, to start drawing, remembering as an artist does; to make more and more drawings—as many as I could, until my memory ran out. I wanted to capture Sandburg in characteristic gestures and aspects that I had not the opportunity to draw on the spot: Sandburg in a barber's chair, smiling broadly after a haircut, with gleaming white hair combed back; Sandburg saying that hated word "exclooooo-sive!"; Sandburg with his shuffling gait, carrying a guitar, cheroot in mouth. Other images flipped into view as the ring of pictures rotated in my memory.

A whole day of this. I felt that as long as I kept drawing Sandburg, I was breathing life into him. Then, visual memory had spun its course. The artist had done all he could do.

Now, my drawing done, having brought Sandburg back to life under my hand, I began to accept the fact of his death.

Facing me among the drawings spread out on my drawing table was the one of Sandburg standing pigeon-toed at my front door, intricately scarved against an early spring chill. His dark hat flopped in the breeze. Slung from his gnarled brown-spotted hand, his shopping bag burst with fruit, books, underwear, socks, and a clean shirt. I could hear his husky baritone. "Helloh-h-h d'Alez-z-zioh-h-h!"

That was my last goodbye thought: Sandburg saying hello.

No Sad Songs

A BUNCH OF THE BOYS and a few girls were whooping it up at the Overseas Press Club, New York, in the fall of 1967, when one of the girls, tossing her tawny tresses back from her finely boned face, said huskily, as only Tallulah Bankhead could say it: "Just the kind of memorial evening Carl Sandburg would have wanted—gay, and no crying."

But the party didn't stay lively and gay for long, not with sentimental girls like Tallulah around, and that other, Fannie Hurst, the inventor of sentimentality. Most of the 200 folk who attended the tribute were Carl's colleagues in the scrivener's trade. Tallulah had struck the keynote of the party: gaiety, no tears. But then, Baritone Bankhead had to break out into song, of course; and down went the waterworks dam. Laughter gave way to tears, just as Sandburg would have wanted it.

Tallulah sang her message to Carl: "I'll be seeing you." The song took on heightened poignancy seventeen months later when Miss Bankhead died.

Sandburg's last birthday was his eighty-ninth. It was not a birthday particularly noted, as had been countless other birthdays in his long life. He was in his dozing period before the big sleep would begin. It was how the family wanted it; he was going easy into the night.

But when his ninetieth birthday rolled around—January 6, 1968—
it was especially marked, Hallmarked, to be precise, by the New York
gallery of the same name, with a mammoth exhibition of photos,
manuscripts, letters, books, cartoons, drawings, and much personal
memorabilia having to do with the poet.

There were no sad songs for Sandburg; all were merry and
rollicking, the kind that Sandburg himself loved to sing. Which he
did sing for the duration of the exhibit, via recordings. The sound of
recorded Sandburg poetry, read by Sandburg, also filled the galleries.
He was everywhere heard and everywhere seen. By far the largest
and most dramatic photo portrayal of Sandburg was the huge blowup
of Edward Steichen's multiple image of the poet, taken in 1939. "The
six shifting phizzogs," Sandburg once described the striking portrait.
Truly, the stop-motion images dwarfed all other representations in the
show, not only in size, but also in dramatic and kinetic impact.

The smallest graphic representation of Sandburg in the exhibit was
a drawing of the poet as troubadour. He is scarved, dark-hatted, dark-
suited, in a pigeon-toed stance, holding a guitar in its case, and taking
a drag at the remains of a cheroot so minuscule that only a thin pen
squiggle above it representing smoke indicates its presence in the
drawing, all of this 5" high, 1½" wide. As for its depth, only I could
feel it, for I had drawn it. Here was Carl Sandburg as he was to me
more than anything else: a man with a guitar.

I looked into every corner of the gallery for other pictures of
Sandburg with guitar and found none.

But the Sandburg guitar was very much in evidence. The real thing
in all the glory of its chosen woods and metals, played a leading role in
a tableau featuring other old, close, and warm friends, inanimate until
Sandburg would give them life by his attention and touch. All of
them were there in Sandburg's workroom-study, lifted from Connemara to Fifth Avenue for the exhibit. There was Carl's old and
battered Eli Whitney cotton gin of a typewriter, with a sheet of paper
rolled into it, waiting, waiting. There was the table, an orange crate;
the famous green eye shade of Sandburg's city-desk days, off to one
side; his press pass; a haggle of hats; a clutch of canes for walking at
Connemara; medals, watches, books, books, and books. The guitar,
one of his oldest and the one he played most at home, was a wire-
string, lyre-shaped Washburn, an American make, resting casually

against an empty chair. The realistic set had a RETURN IN FIFTEEN MINUTES look. I waited until I could believe that Carl would actually shuffle in from a tramp around the farm, hook his hat on the rack, restore his walking stick to its place with the others, pick up his guitar, and sing a song that had come to him during his walk. Then, he would go to his typewriter atop the orange crate and start fulfilling the expectations of the blank paper, waiting, waiting . . .

The Washington services for Sandburg had been knee-deep in dignitaries; the Overseas Press Club bash was a crush of cronies. Now came along the handsome Hallmark tribute. It ran for two months. Sandburg's family had officially opened the show. His wife and daughters came up from Connemara, and Edward Steichen and his wife, Joanna, came down from Connecticut. Now there was plenty of time for the rest of Sandburg's friends—especially those who had been "family" to him across the years—to see, to hear, to touch; to marvel at this miracle of electronic, technological achievement, combined with the human ingredients of imagination and taste, stopping short only at actual resurrection of America's Bard.

Yes, the Hallmark people knew their business, all right. They knew how to put together a birthday card.

In the early 1940s, just after Sandburg completed his *Abraham Lincoln: The War Years,* he promptly won the Pulitzer Prize for history. He was still reeling from the mean rigors of the lonely, monumental task, and the strain from bearing so awesome a responsibility—a poet turned historian. It was time for a change.

The four-volume work, a million words, was conceived and written in a small cottage nestled among the sand dunes at Harbert, Michigan, by the Great Lake of the same name. The Sandburgs went to Harbert first for the summers, and then chose to make their year-round residence there. Harbert was a popular lake resort, and summers there were a joy. But the winters were brutal. An icy wind always cut across lake and dune and with a brazen ease crept into crevices of house and joints of bone. Aside from the physical discomforts at the Harbert home, there was one even more pressing, and steadily increasing: Paula's herd of championship dairy goats, straining, constricted, and demanding more open space. There was an even more tender reason to get into another clime and place: fond father Carl's desire to grant daughter Helga's wistful dream of a farm and horses. It was indeed time for a change.

Without further delay, and with Carl's blessing, three ladies of the Sandburg family—Paula, Helga, and Dana Steichen, Ed Steichen's second wife—set out to find a new home. They found it in 1945 and that year they made the move to Connemara Farm in Flat Rock, North Carolina. The sunny white farm house on Little Glassy Mountain was to be Carl's last home.

He left Lincoln country and the house where he had lived and agonized with Old Abe through *The War Years*. This mammoth job of writing took him three times as long to finish as the Civil War took to be fought from Bull Run to Appomattox Court House.

As an historian, it was incumbent upon Sandburg to write dispassionately of the Confederacy. But of course, as a champion of freedom and human rights, his deep sentiments all bore the Union label. Where else, in a struggle against human slavery, would Carl Sandburg's heart be? His cause was Lincoln's cause and the cause of the North. From birth to his sixty-seventh year, the North, particularly Lincoln's Middle West, had been his stamping grounds.

But now the South was getting him for the rest of his days. Carl Sandburg of the North, an abolitionist, an extension of Abraham Lincoln, became Carl Sandburg of the landed gentry of the South, comfortably established in Confederate territory for the next twenty-two years of his life. Some move! Sandburg's sand dunes in Michigan would soon become a memory. Now he had 245 acres of Carolina woodland where he could walk, raise goats, keep horses, watch birds, and work in solitude.

Christopher Gustavus Memminger, secretary of the treasury in Jefferson Davis's Confederate cabinet, built the house which the Sandburgs acquired. Memminger was a South Carolinian via Wurtemburg, Germany, brought to the United States around 1804 as an infant. He attained several positions of prominence in the Confederacy, winding up as its treasury chief. Needing a summer home to escape the city heat of Charleston, South Carolina, he built Rock Hill, later called Connemara Farm by a subsequent owner, on land located in western North Carolina.

Thus Carl came to Connemara to live in a house first owned by the keeper of the Confederate dollar, which could only be purchased now with hard Yankee dollars. The two masters of the house were a hundred years apart in time; their 245 acres commanded a beautiful view 2,300 feet above sea level, amid the Appalachians and the Blue Ridge near Hendersonville, North Carolina. Memminger the Southerner came to Flat Rock to cool off; Sandburg the Northerner came to warm up!

The Sandburg guitar always found honor in his own home, with his whole family and with Paula Sandburg especially. She knew all about her husband's romance with the guitar. More than that, she, too, loved it for his loving it.

She was careful to preserve the cherished collection of guitars which he had left behind. There were four of them always resting around the house like old family pets, and about two years after Carl's death, Paula noted with alarm that they needed repair. In a year or so she realized they would figure prominently as exhibits when Connemara Farm would be thrown open to the public by the National Park Service as an historic site—a vivid and living monument to the American poet. The home, the grounds, the goats, the farm, everything, would be frozen "as is." The Sandburg ladies would just pack and go without so much as throwing a sheet over armchair or sofa. Paula was especially anxious about the guitars. In the sound box of each one, the songs of Sandburg were still ringing, and before she turned them over to the Park Service, they had to be in prime condition along with every other detail, item, and artifact of Sandburgiana—from memo pad to stump of cheroot to the goats on the farm of the 245-acre estate.

The day of the Park Service take-over was fast approaching, and the guitars still awaited attention. Late in June 1969, Paula appealed to Sophocles Papas for help in the rehabilitation of the instruments, knowing that he could fill any guitar need, pedagogical, mechanical, historical, cultural. Along with her SOS was her invitation to Sophocles and his Missus Mercia to stay the night at Connemara in Carl's very own bedroom. More than ten years before, Carl, house guest then at the Papas home, was thrilled to have slept in the "same bed Segovia slept in." Now Sandburg, posthumously, could return the hospitality of his erstwhile host.

Well in advance of the day in 1969 when Paula Sandburg relinquished ownership of Connemara Farm to the National Park Service, the four guitars in Papas's charge were ready for delivery. They were not only in playing shape, but also in displaying shape for their new role as museum pieces.

After twenty-two years and thousands of good memories, it was time to say farewell to Connemara. The Sandburg ladies—Paula and daughters Janet and Margaret—moved from Connemara to nearby Asheville, North Carolina.

The Sandburg guitars would remain under the reverent protection of Papas until the Connemara Museum was ready to receive them.

Soon the public would see these lifelong companions of Carl Sandburg: a six-string guitar lute, newish, German-made; a small wire-string Washburn guitar about fifty years old; a Vega guitar, at least fifty years old, also with wire strings and metal tailpiece, and a modern classic guitar made in Spain—no label.

There were other Sandburg guitars, of course, those beautiful examples by master luthiers that he had acquired over the years. None of those could be shown at Connemara, simply because the Old Troubadour gave them away to people he loved who loved the guitar.

Epilogue

Some Laughter Is Better Than Slumber

EVEN IF YOU NEVER HEARD of Jean Cocteau, master of the paradox, poet, playwright, painter, you would have the key to his life and style and persona from the answer he once gave to a question in the course of an interview.

The answer was: "The fire."

The question was, "If your house were on fire, and you were granted the wish to save only one thing from it, what would you save?"

That was the name of the game we were playing one evening late in the fall of 1967. We were a diverse group, but a common bond kept us together: our love for the guitar. We were the New York guitar crowd that Carl Sandburg had discovered almost twenty years earlier. Three months had passed since Carl died, and we were gathered together at my house on Henderson Place to eat, drink, play, sing, talk—and remember our friend the Old Troubadour who used to preside over the fun, festivities, and music in this room.

It was October and chilly. We were seated comfortably in a semicircle before a crackling fire. Silently, we contemplated the flames. Tethered and contained, the fire was enacting obediently its role as servant of man.

Obviously, this was not the tamed, domestic animal that Cocteau would save, I was thinking. Should the fire make a dash for freedom from its three-walled confinement and run wild and unchecked through the house, what would I save from the flames?

My lofty first thought was my guitar. But what about that portfolio upstairs with all those valuable papers? My paintings? Or several pieces of jewelry we had in a drawer someplace? Or one of my drawings of Sandburg? Not easy to play, this game.

I threw open the floor to the fire game, first giving the question as put to Cocteau, but withholding his answer until all of ours were in.

As expected from so diverse a group, the answers that tumbled forth varied. Emmett, our cynical, always financially uptight friend, would save nothing. "I'd let the damn house burn down and collect the insurance!" he said quickly and without the blink of an eye.

Only one person of the dozen of us would choose his guitar—his magnificent irreplaceable Ramirez, but this was not altogether a choice of the heart; he was a professional, and the guitar was his livelihood. Though we all loved our guitars, the loss of an instrument would be no tragedy or trauma for the rest of us. Our love was for the romance of the guitar, which no fire could destroy.

Rare books, jewelry, furs, documents, objects d'art—these were the nature of the choices, all inherently materialistic. Knowing Cocteau's transcendental answer, I cautiously withheld my own; I would wait upon Terry's. Hers would be mine. From that June day in 1938 when I said "I do" in *the little church around the corner,* she has been my altar ego.

At this point, I sprung the Cocteau choice. My friends laughed, gasped, frowned, guffawed, puzzled over it, some of them sure it was apocryphal at best, but more likely nothing more than a Cocteau-and-bull story. Then I launched into my "lecture": true or not, the story plainly pointed up a moral. Though nihilistic on its surface, the deep significance of Cocteau's choice was the insignificance of material possessions and man's preoccupation with their false values. Sooner or later comes the fire, at once destroying and purifying. Everyone nodded sagely, but I doubted they bought my interpretation.

I hadn't given my choice, nor had Terry, someone pointed out. What was holding us up? I said I meant to go along with Terry's answer, whatever it would be; she was the brains and the conscience of the family. What would she save? All attention turned to Terry the Wise.

She sat looking into the fire, stroking the head of her dog, Shawgee. Somebody said, "I know what Terry'd save—her dog!"

She answered indignantly, "Shawgee is not a *what;* he's a *who,* and according to the rule, *who's* are not allowed."

"What would you save then?" asked another. I could tell by her gravely set face that this was no frivolous party-game question for her.

"I have many, many things that are personally very precious to me," Terry mused, "but if I were to consider them as really and seriously significant, I guess I would just have to sit the fire out—in the house, I mean—and go with it, because it would be impossible to save everything that seems important to me. So much for the material things. The fire? I'd fight it to the end. Ashes don't look like rebirth to me. I would destroy it to keep it from destroying this room we're sitting in and the treasure it holds, not only for me, but for all of us. It's here all around us, even now. The fun, the laughter when Sandburg was with us. Remember that crazy party when a neighbor complained about the racket we were making, and what Carl said . . ."

We all remembered. We all chorused, "Some laughter is better than slumber."

Terry said, "That's what I would save in this house: the laughter."

Index

Index